Routledge Revivals

Towards Economic Freedom

Towards Economic Freedom (1937) presents the fundamentals of economics in their historical perspective, and reduces economic theory to its simplest terms. The common human need for food, clothing and shelter is evident to all, and the business of production and distribution should be available for study to all.

Towards Economic Freedom

An Outline of World Economic History

Helen Corke

Routledge Revivals
Routledge
Taylor & Francis Group

First published in 1937
by Methuen & Co. Ltd.

This edition first published in 2025 by Routledge
4 Park Square, Milton Park, Abingdon, Oxon, OX14 4RN

and by Routledge
605 Third Avenue, New York, NY 10017

Routledge is an imprint of the Taylor & Francis Group, an informa business

A Library of Congress record exists under LCCN: 39016308

ISBN: 978-1-041-00826-2 (hbk)
ISBN: 978-1-003-61185-1 (ebk)
ISBN: 978-1-041-00827-9 (pbk)

Book DOI 10.4324/9781003611851

TOWARDS ECONOMIC FREEDOM

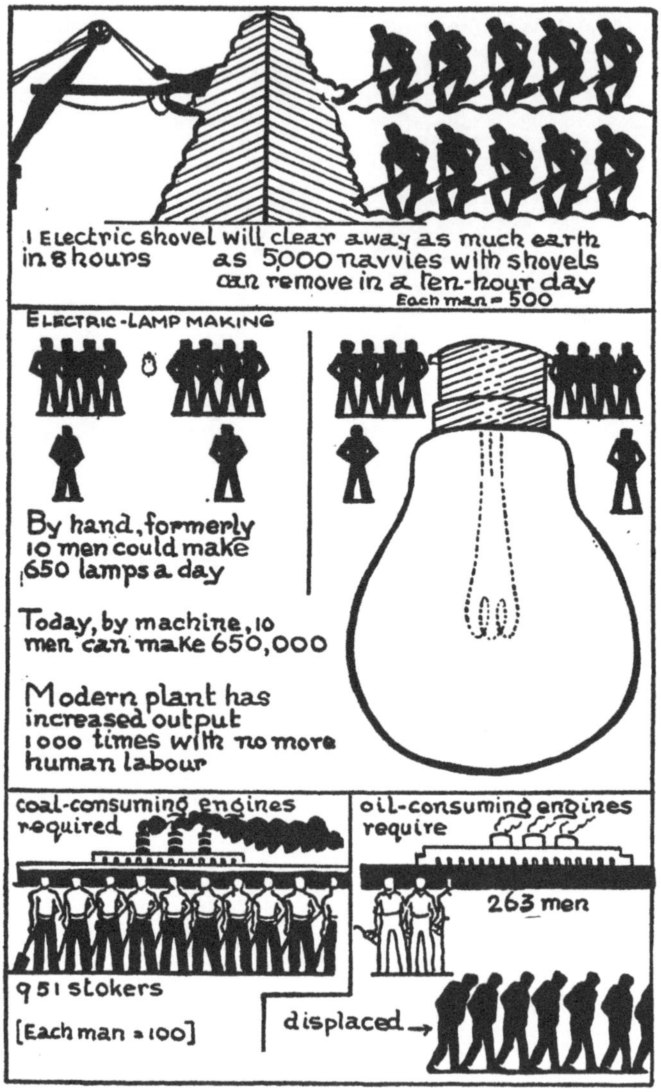

DISPLACEMENT OF LABOUR—1

TOWARDS ECONOMIC FREEDOM

An Outline of World Economic History

by

HELEN CORKE

Illustrated with pictorial statistics

by

WILMA HICKSON

LONDON: METHUEN & CO. LTD.

36 Essex Street, Strand, W.C.2

By the Same Author

THE CLASS BOOKS OF WORLD HISTORY

- I. The World's Family
- II. The Home Builders
- III. The Adventurers
- IV. Mankind the Conqueror.

A BOOK OF ANCIENT PEOPLES

A BOOK OF MODERN PEOPLES

FROM SCARCITY TO PLENTY
A Short Course of Economic History,
(16th to 20th Centuries).

First published in 1937

PRINTED IN GREAT BRITAIN

PREFACE

THIS little book endeavours to present the fundamentals of economics in their historical perspective, and to reduce economic theory to its simplest terms. The common human need for food, clothing, shelter, is evident to the least sophisticated; so might be, so should be, the means whereby the need is met. In the past this business of production and distribution, and especially the part which finance plays in the matter, has been set aside as a study for the expert—heaven knows *why*, since there is no subject which more closely concerns every ordinary citizen. The approach through history (as distinct from that through classic theory) offers no difficulty either to the schoolboy or to the erstwhile puzzled student of modern economic conditions.

A book of this type, like a modern machine, owes less to its constructor than to those workers on whose thought he builds. I dedicate it, in gratitude, to all whose earlier, more intensive labours in the field of economic history have made mine possible. My thanks are due to Sir Norman Angell, Dr. Hendrik van Loon, Miss C. M. Waters, Sir Leonard Woolley, and their respective publishers for quotations used; also to the illustrator, Miss Wilma Hickson, for her indispensable part in the book's production.

H.C.

CONTENTS

DIAGRAMS

INTRODUCTION

ECONOMICS means 'house-keeping,' in the sense of properly supplying the household need. The business of providing a family or a community with its day to day requirements is a continuous one, effective and satisfactory only when it is carried on regularly, and in relation to the family's or community's power to use or consume the goods provided. If the supply is spasmodic, irregular, or unrelated to the need, it is unsatisfactory.

A house-keeper procuring on the first day of the month butter or meat enough to last her family till its end would be acting (unless the house had unusual facilities for cold storage) in an *un-economic* manner, for much of the food would be wasted. The same would be true were she to buy, for a family normally consuming a loaf of bread per day, three loaves on Monday, and no more until Friday; or bacon, no matter how cheap, if members of the family could not digest it. Her house-keeping is good, or *economical*, if she procures the food and other commodities needed by each member of the household when required, and in such quantity as to avoid waste.

One other point we note here. Each individual has varying personal needs. The good house-keeper distributes commodities according to those needs. It would be most uneconomical for her to provide Jack, aged two, with salmon and cucumber for lunch, while setting only milk-food before his father; nor would George, the fifteen-year-old school-boy, be satisfied with Aunt Dorothy's breakfast of thin toast.

The term *Economics* is used to mean the study of the world's house-keeping. That is to say, the study of the ways and means by which we, as individuals, obtain our particular share of the world's produce. Used in this sense, note that it means 'house-keeping' merely—not *good* house-keeping. It will be necessary for us to examine these ways and means before we can say whether they are good or no.

Each of us needs *things*. The things we need for the body, the essentials of our physical existence, are of three kinds—food, clothing and shelter with warmth. These primary needs are the same as those of men in the Early Stone Age—they never change. It is the nature and variety of the food, clothing and shelter which changes.

We know that our primitive ancestors fed on the flesh of the smaller wild animals and birds, on wild roots and berries; that they sheltered in caves and pits and wrapped themselves in skins. As far back as the remote age of these Palæolithic Men our study of Economics begins, and even then the task of food-getting was *shared*. Two men hunting together were less at the mercy of forest beasts, and more likely to secure their prey, than a single hunter. Each member of a family would use his or her individual skill, for stone-throwing, for swift running, for the shaping of darts, etc., in the common task of securing food enough for all. A tribe, uniting in effort, might succeed in trapping and killing a sick mammoth, thus providing a plenitude of food for the whole community. As in such ways Stone Age Man displayed *association for labour*,[1] so we may also trace an early *division of labour*.[2] One of the most ancient of Egyptian picture-records, made nearly 6,000 years ago, shows the various processes by which crude ore and blue stone are transformed into an elegant gold and lapis-lazuli jar; these processes are shared among many workers.

[1]See Note 1 [2]See Note 2

Stone Age man led a precarious existence. Always he faced the two problems, *how to get food, and how to escape being eaten.* If he were relatively strong, active, cunning, he was not often hungry. He killed, he ate. If the prey were large, he ate largely, and conversely, he could fast long without becoming exhausted. But a rigorous winter or a long drought might mean scarcity of food for man and beast, and a serious decrease in the human population. Those who survived such a time of stress did so either on account of a greater capacity for endurance than their kin, or because they had *stored* food. Gradually the will to store, to save, to accumulate food became an inherited instinct in the mind of man. Impressed by habit, by custom, and later by proverb and precept, by the practice of countless generations, it emerged eventually as a *moral* idea. To save was better than to consume, or more precisely, to save was *right*, to consume more than sheer necessity demanded was *wrong*.

The Old Stone Age hunter had small chance of storing surplus food. The Newer Stone Age (Neolithic) races began to breed domestic animals and to cultivate corn; from their time onward men have accumulated and hoarded wealth—*wealth* in its true sense of things useful and serviceable to man. The carcass brought home by the hunter could be kept only a brief time, but the shepherd's flock was potential food and clothing for future months and years. A hoard of wild nuts and berries might sustain a hunter's family through a winter; but well-sown corn would (apart from evil chance) increase itself many-fold.

When mankind had acquired the power to accumulate wealth two results followed. One was the division of human communities into *rich* and *poor*; the other was the necessity which arose for the *exchange of products*.

Primarily it was the careful shepherd, the good farmer, who became rich. But secondarily, and as certainly, it was the strong and ruthless robber. To tend sheep and cattle, to grow corn, was good, but useless, failing the means of *defending* such wealth. The wealthy tribe must needs be the tribe best furnished with armed defenders. And given the tribe's desire for increasing wealth, how easy for the defenders to become assailants, turning their weapons against other tribes for the purpose of capturing their possessions! So stored wealth engendered warfare, and the poor man or tribe is seen to be, henceforward, not only he who has failed through lack of industry or intelligence to accumulate stocks, but the vanquished in battle.

The alternative to the seizure of another's goods was *barter*. It might happen that one tribe had accumulated great surplus of hides, wool or corn, another woven cloths or spices. Without the risk that attended warfare an exchange could be made. Thus *trade* began, circulating and extending the use of varying kinds of wealth.

Turning to the means used by man to supply himself with food, clothing and shelter, we find the history of *tools* stretching back to the Stone Age. As Dr. Van Loon says, the Old Stone man who first raised a large stone by inserting under it a pointed stick, invented the lever. The useful stick! it flew from his hand and brought down the bird for his meal, it poked the fire that roasted the meal; smoothed and shaped, it formed the shaft of his arrow, the handle of his axe, or bent to form his bow. Still more useful flint and antler, that in various shapes cut and pierced, dug and hewed, in his developing hands.

Each new tool invented, each happy combination of tools resulting in the construction of a *machine* reduced the amount of physical strength the worker needed to exert in achieving his task, lessened the time taken to do it, or increased the efficiency with which it was executed.

But the tool could do nothing of itself; it required driving and directing power. Palæolithic fathers showed their sons how to handle the flint axe and drive it into the tree-trunk; Palæolithic mothers taught their daughters the craft of the bone needle and the spinning whorl of baked clay. Long before the end of the Stone Age in Europe men learned that many hands make light work and that union is strength. Hence the desire for many sons and daughters which is reflected so often in the earlier Hebrew records. As long as their strength lasted the father and mother directed the labours of the family. The physical strength, energy and skill of each member contributed to the common wealth. Each represented a unit of labour force.

The Neolithic tribe (paralleled roughly in our own day by the Bedouin Arab dwellers of the Arabian oases) was a community of related families. Its strength lay in its numbers, for these formed the measure of its working and fighting power. This power was best increased by a high birthrate, for sons and daughters whose interests were bound up with those of the tribe might be expected to serve it willingly. But captives could be compelled to labour, if not to fight, and when this fact had been established in the human mind, slavery began.

It is presumed that the earliest tribal victories were followed by the ritual sacrifice of the male captives to the tribal gods. When it became recognised that the labour of a captive was a tribal asset and that the slave's labour value in terms of the wealth he helped to produce exceeded what he consumed, captured men and women became regarded as commodities. Thereafter, throughout the course of the early civilisations, wealth was estimated in terms of flocks and herds, the produce of the soil, metals, and *slaves*.

Turning to the first pages of historical record, those of Egypt and Sumer nearly 6,000 years ago, we find a tale of settled communities with populations part freemen, part slaves. The freemen are rich and poor, the rich being those who have acquired land, with all its potentialities of pastoral, agricultural and mineral wealth, while the poor are landless men, lacking possessions, and compelled to sell their labour for a wage whereby they may live. The wage is not necessarily money; it may be dole of food and clothing, shelter or house-room, or perhaps claim to a piece of cultivable land. The poor freeman who must sell the whole of his working time and strength to another differs from the slave only in that he cannot be compelled by his master to labour; he may beg, he may leave the community and take to the life of the outlaw hunter in unclaimed desert or forest. One other course is open to the poor freeman—he may hire himself out as a fighter instead of as a worker, in which case the justice of his king's cause will matter less to him than the fighting wage he is promised, or the chance of loot.

Let us then begin with primitive man, able only to *seize* and *consume* the products of nature, like the animals his fellows. We will watch him as his increasing intelligence enables him to assist in the process of natural production, and to utilise more products. We note his early tendencies to hoard wealth, to defend his hoards, and his first efforts to facilitate exchange and distribution of goods. We shall presently see how, from his crude beginnings, the economic system of our modern world has grown.

PART I

THE ERA OF PHYSICAL ENERGY AND HUMAN LABOUR

CHAPTER I

ECONOMICS IN ANCIENT EGYPT AND BABYLONIA

ALONG the river valleys of the Nile and the Euphrates diggers in search of ancient things have discovered the sites of towns and villages which were centres of civilisation 5,000 to 6,000 years ago. Careful investigation of these sites has shown what food was eaten, what clothing worn, and what materials and objects were used by these early peoples.

The Old Stone Age hunters were nomads, following the herds of wild reindeer or horses in their yearly migration from summer to winter feeding grounds. The New Stone Age herdsmen were also nomads, whose wanderings were determined by the needs of their flocks and herds. Nomads must carry their goods with them wherever they go, and this fact limited the nomad tribesman's desire for possessions to such simple objects as served his daily use and satisfied his love of adornment. Only when he ceased to travel, and settled down to live in some desirable 'land of milk and honey' did he begin to accumulate stores of food and clothing, and to develop to the pitch of excellence his natural arts and crafts. Then, also, he replaced his skin tent or reed hut by a dwelling of beaten clay and sundried brick, or in timbered country by a log cabin.

Men settled early in the Nile Valley, where barley, millet and wheat grew wild, as grasses. The first Egyptians chewed the seeds, stored them in clay pots, noticed how they germinated and grew if dropped into the earth. Eventually these settlers began the deliberate cultivation of corn. Centuries rolled slowly by until the time came when the rich, corn-bearing lands of Egypt drew towards them the shepherd tribes of Canaan and Syria and the desert dwellers of Nubia and Arabia. Barns and granaries full of corn ensured men and domestic animals against starvation the whole year through. For tribes thus provided, hunting might become a pastime instead of a necessary occupation. Their people could spend the energy formerly devoted to searching for prey, on finding ways and means of increasing their wealth (the word means goods and possessions in general, not money), and what was equally essential, ways and means of defending it against raiders. The mighty hunter, hero of the most primitive tribal legends, began to rank second in honour to the indomitable warrior, while the actual *producers* of the wealth, farmer, shepherd, craftsman, came to be regarded by the tribal mind as inferior in caste to its *defenders*. It was not that the producers *were* inferior to the defenders—but glittering weapons, strident challenge, an assumption of power to take and to keep, all made and still make a direct appeal to simple and primitive people.

Meanwhile, to his knowledge of the uses of stone, the early Egyptian had added a knowledge of the uses of *copper* and *gold*. Copper ore was probably used first as a cosmetic or paint, being ground and mixed with resin. Later, some chance showed observers what happened when ore was heated in the fire; and then the smelting and shaping of copper began. Hammered copper produced a tool or weapon easier to manipulate, because lighter, than one of flint, and, polished, it gave back a ruddy gleam pleasing to the eye. But copper took, presently, a second place to *gold*.

Gold was found in shining nuggets among the sands

of the Nubian desert.[1] More pure than copper, it seemed to partake of the sun's nature, and mingle with his rays. The early Egyptians believed that Ra, the Sun-god, drew the living plant from the dry, dead grain, and they worshipped him as Lord of Existence, Father of All. Hence the shining metal became to them the symbol of Ra, his seed, and the peculiar and fit possession of the king, whom the Egyptian priesthood taught was the Son of Ra. Lesser men than those of the royal house wore gold charms or amulets, magic things they seemed, that being of the nature of god, would ward away evil from their owners. Thus began to grow in the mind of man that reverence for and desire to possess *gold* which persists to our own day.

Lower Egypt, the Nile delta, was an expanse of rich, alluvial soil, covered, in a wild state, by jungle, and intersected by slow streams. Upper Egypt was the rift valley, between limestone cliffs, along which the river runs for 600 miles above the present city of Cairo. Human tribal groups had settled in this delta and valley more than 6,000 years ago; these were the earliest Egyptians, hunters, using flint knives and axes, dwelling in reed huts, storing the wild grain in their rough pottery. Many centuries passed; they hunted less and dug more, extending their cultivation of corn along the valley. Thus pushing outwards from their original settlements, the tribes came into conflict, stronger tribe defeating weaker tribe, seizing its land and possessions, enslaving a portion of its people, placing its tribal god image in the shrine of the victor's deity. Eventually we read of a single powerful tribe, that of the king Menes, dominating the whole of Egypt, and so the long history of the Pharaoh-civilisation begins.

The barley, millet and wheat were sown by slaves or poor freemen in the warm black Nile mud, while the flood was receding. The growing corn could be watered

[1]Breasted, *Ancient Times.*

only by irrigation, since no rain falls in Egypt, and the little trench or ditch dug by the pre-historic villager to drain the river water to his corn patch is widened and deepened by his descendants, till in the time of the First Dynasty the Bahr Yusef Canal runs for 300 miles, marking the boundary of the irrigated land.[1] At harvesting, each lord's steward receives from the overseers and tenant farmers the tale of the grain which, less the shares of the priesthood and the Pharaoh, fills his lord's barns.

Up and down the Nile pass the slave-rowed barges bringing, from Sudan in the south, ebony, ivory, ostrich plumes and fragrant gums—or from the Delta papyrus and wool—all to be exchanged for corn. By the Syrian and Red Sea border caravan routes come gold, coral, copper, cedar-wood, cloth from the looms of Babylonian towns in the Euphrates valley. The fertility of Egypt's soil, and the labour of the slaves and poor freemen, ensure a life of leisure for the Egyptian land-owners, the priesthood, and the court; food, clothing and shelter are secured to them in abundance—they 'toil not, neither do they spin.' When the energy of men is released from the task of providing these prime necessities, it can occupy itself in the search for knowledge (geographical and scientific discovery), in invention, in all forms of creative art, in the further acquisition of wealth or power, and in philosophical and religious speculation.

All these occupations interested the Egyptians, but they gave a special attention to the last-named. Their ideas concerning the soul led them to build the immense pyramid tombs which Pharaohs of the Third Dynasty raised in the desert, and which remain to-day, the oldest remaining buildings in existence. The larger pyramids were formed of rough-hewn stone blocks, space being left, between internal walls, for the construction of one

[1]Myres, *The Dawn of History*.

or more vaulted chambers. Massive blocks of hewn stone, finely jointed, cased the pyramids; the stone was sawn by copper saws fed with emery powder[1]—but no one can say how these blocks, some weighing thirty tons, were conveyed from their distant quarries and hoisted into place. The work done on the pyramids is the more amazing when we note that stone was not ordinarily used in Egypt for house or temple building. Temples were hewn from the rock of the cliffs; houses, even the palaces, were built of wood. It is interesting to note that many of the tools in common use among the ancient Egyptians have persisted into modern times with very little variation upon their original form.

While thus mankind developed by the Nile between 4000 and 1000 B.C., similar developments were taking place in the delta of the rivers Euphrates and Tigris, and in the plateau region of their upper courses. Here again, in the delta, alluvial soil of great fertility brought forth grain and fruit in wild abundance: fish, fowl and small game were plentiful, and tribes settled, turning from a nomad life to the possession and cultivation of land. Like the Egyptians, they sowed the seed of the wild barley, and cut their harvest with sickles of baked clay. They made clay pots and painted them; they used bone awls and netting needles; they fished from canoes made of reeds caulked with clay. But these primitive folk also possessed things which they must have gained by barter—flint knives, copper saws, stone sockets for the hinge poles of their reed and clay huts, necklaces of crystal and cornelian beads. There was no flint native to the delta, nor any stone or metal.[2]

When decipherable written records begin, they tell of a people who came from the eastward into this region, which, after their coming, is called *Sumer*. The Sumerians build great clay mounds as foundations for their temples—artificial hills preserving the temples from

[1]Flinders Petrie, *Encyc. Britt*, Article on Egypt. [2]Woolley, *The Sumerians*.

inundation by the frequent river floods. Their settlements are made around the temples; the 'holy hill' is thus a place of refuge for them and their beasts in flood-time. Such 'cities' were Ur and Babylon, Kish, Lagash and others. Each developed as an independent state, governed by the chief priest (patesi) of its temple. As in Egypt, these tribal groups came often into conflict. About 2630 B.C. *Lagash* was raided by the men of *Umma*; on this occasion a priest of the vanquished city wrote a lament, using wedge-shaped pencil on tablet of moist clay:

> "*They have shed blood in the shrine of Enlil and in the shrine of the Sun-god,*
> *They have carried away the silver and the precious stones, and have destroyed the statue. . . .*
> *They have removed the grain from Ginarbaniru, from the field of Ningirsu,*
> *All of it that was under cultivation.*"[1]

His clay tablet lay buried among the ruins of the city until archæologists of our own century discovered it, and owing to the similarity between ancient Sumerian and the later Persian script were able to translate the lament.

An examination of the royal tombs, both of Egypt and Sumer, has shown materials and objects used by the peoples of these early civilisations. The personal possessions of the dead were commonly buried with them. At Ur were found gold and silver bowls, daggers and lamps, beautifully chased, a golden helmet, rings, necklaces, bracelets and head-dresses of gold, silver and lapis-lazuli beads. There were fine socketed axes of copper and electrum, and beautiful inlaid mosaic work in shell and mother-of-pearl. Clearly the craftsmen of those far-off days had attained a pitch of excellence in

[1]Woolley.

their various handicrafts that can scarcely be exceeded in our own. The Sumerian objects give evidence of a lively foreign trade, as Sir Leonard Woolley points out:

> "Not the least interesting point about the treasures recovered from the site of Ur is that the raw material of nearly all of them is imported from abroad. Bitumen was brought down river from Hit, then Subartu-land; copper came from Oman, as is shown by the analysis of the ores, and probably also from the Caucasus; silver from Bulgar Maden in northern Cilicia and from the hills of south Elam; gold may have been imported from Elam, from Cappadocia, and from the Antioch region of Syria."[1]

Sir Leonard Woolley instances many more of the products which must, in his opinion, have been traded to the people of Ur, and then continues:

> "Lastly, there are found in Egypt, about the time of the First Dynasty there . . . certain products which are unmistakably borrowed from Mesopotamia: stone mace-heads, cylinder seals, stone vase shapes, and the panelled decoration of walls; and such borrowings denote at least a trade connexion with the Euphrates valley."[2]

We may conclude therefore that, at least 5,000 years ago, in these two regions so favourable to man's development, the valleys of the Nile and the Euphrates, food was grown, clothing woven, building carried on, as satisfactorily as at any time of later date previous to the discovery of steam-power. Also that the products of these and other regions were distributed by barter or some other system of exchange.

[1]The Sumerians. [2]The Sumerians.

Another thousand years passes. In 1950 B.C. that remarkable king, HAMMURABI OF BABYLON was ruling the whole of Sumer, and Accad, the province to its north. The British Museum possesses a large number of letters, written on clay tablets and enclosed in clay envelopes, which originally circulated between the king and various officials occupied with the administration of the kingdom. These letters, together with the temple records—the great store granaries were within the temple precincts—tell us much about the economic life of that age. We learn that silver, measured by weight, was used as money; houses and land being bought and sold for silver, though barter was the common way of trading commodities. Houses and land were commonly held by *lease*, as now. Loans of corn, silver, etc., were made at interest; if the loan were corn, it had to be returned by a stated date, with additional measure for interest. Every business agreement between merchant and merchant, or between merchant and buyer, had to be recorded on a clay tablet and sealed.

Three *castes* or classes of Babylonian society were recognised. The highest included priests, government officials and soldiers; the middle comprised the merchants, farmers, labourers and artisans; the lowest were slaves. These last were prisoners of war, persons born of slave parents, or persons reduced to slavery as a punishment. Parents could sell sons or daughters as slaves. Yet a slave might, if permitted by his master, own goods, engage in trade, or gain by any legal means the money to buy his freedom.

In this chapter, be it noted, we have briefly surveyed a long tract of human evolution—in all over 7,000 years. Between King Hammurabi's time and our own stretch 3,880 years, a little more than half that time. We can now summarise the facts relating to the production and distribution of goods and services towards the end of this long earlier period, within which man developed, century by century, the habits and customs of an economic practice from which all later systems have been derived.

Production and Distribution before 2000 B.C.

PRODUCTION

Agricultural. The tilling of soil with spade and ox-plough; digging of ditches and canals for irrigation purposes; cultivation of grain, fruit and vegetables; planting and felling of trees; making of gardens.

Industrial. The use of wood, stone, clay, and the metals copper, bronze, electrum, gold and silver. The manufacture (hand) of *tools*—dibber, spade, simple plough; in Egypt the shaduf for raising water; most of the mason's and carpenter's tools in similar form to those in modern use; and (in Sumer) the wheel. The brush and wedge-shaped pencil for writing. The lever.

The building of brick and wood dwellings; making of chairs, beds and other furniture; hewing of tombs and temples from rock-face; construction of stone pyramids and monuments.

The spinning of woollen and linen thread (with spinning whorl) weaving of cloth (hand-loom); fulling and dyeing thread and cloth; tanning of hides for leather; shoe and harness making; pottery and jewellery work.

DISTRIBUTION

(*a*) The exchange of surplus goods between man and man and also between merchants of different countries. The transport of such goods across long distances of desert and forest by ass and camel caravan; also along shores of Persian Gulf and Mediterranean Sea by sailing or rowing boats.

(*b*) The use of silver ***by weight*** as money. The inscribing and sealing of business agreements.

(*c*) The sale in open market and by private agreement of houses, land, slaves, cattle, commodities, goods and services.

CHAPTER II

IN ASIATIC LANDS: JUDÆA; INDIA; CHINA

THE Jews were originally a pastoral people.

Their Old Testament records illustrate more than 1,500 years of Hebrew and Jewish life in the little land now called Palestine. Lying between the greater nations of Egypt and Babylonia its people could not maintain their independence as a separate people politically—they were always subject to the rule of the Egyptian or Babylonian overlord and compelled to pay tribute. When there was war between these two powers, Palestine was the battle-ground. Yet, though Jerusalem were besieged and looted, and its king and court exiled, as in the time of the prophet *Jeremiah*, the majority of the Hebrew farmers continued to live on their small farms, shearing their sheep and pruning their vines, ploughing, sowing and reaping in season, more concerned with weather changes than with changes of government. If the rains did not fail, if the harvest were safely gathered and garnered, if the tax-collector left them enough of their produce to support their families in reasonable plenty till the next harvest, life was as satisfactory for them as they could expect it to be. Their part in trade was limited to an exchange of surplus commodities with their neighbours, and to occasional barter with the merchants of Babylonian or Egyptian caravans halting on the confines of their land. "The ideal of the Israelite was to repose in the shade of his own fig tree—not to have a large number of figs to trade with."[1]

[1]J. Jacobs, *Jewish Contribution to Civilisation.*

The economic ideas of the Jews were closely related to their religious conceptions. YAHWEH, the Supreme, was Lord of Earth and Heaven; therefore all land belonged in the first and last instance to Him. "*The land shall not be sold forever, for the land is Mine,*" said the Jewish priestly law as re-stated after the Exile.[1] The holders of land were therefore the tenants of the Deity. Sons inherited the lands of their fathers; if daughters inherited they were expected to marry their cousins of the same tribe, so that the inheritance should not pass to strangers. At each fiftieth year, the Year of Jubilee,[2] all land which had been sold, together with the buildings placed thereon, was to revert to the original owners. This system of Jewish economy also prescribed that every seventh year should be a year of rest for the soil; it should not then be ploughed or sown, but lie fallow—the owners living upon previously stored grain and the natural yield of fruit. The seventh or Sabbatical year released the debtor from the demands of his creditor. Debts contracted during the six years could not be lawfully claimed in or after the Sabbatical year.

Jewish weights and measures were based on those of ancient Babylonia. Money was *silver*, by weight, the standard weight being the *shekel.* A merchant carried balances and weights at his girdle.

The Law condemned the practice of usury, the seizure by creditors of debtors' land or goods, and the accumulation of many holdings in the hands of the wealthy few. Its key-notes were justice as between man and man, and mercy from the stronger towards the weaker. It maintained the principle of the need for rest and leisure.

"*Ye shall do no unrighteousness in judgment, in meteyard, in weight or in measure. Just balances, just weights, a just ephah and a just hin*[3] *shall ye have.*[4]

[1]Lev. 25. [2]Lev. 25. [3]See Note. [4]Lev. 19.

> "*If thou lend money to any of my people that is poor, thou shalt not be to him as a usurer, neither shalt thou lay upon him usury. If thou take thy neighbour's raiment to pledge, thou shalt deliver it to him by that the sun goeth down.*"[1]

The record in the Book of Kings of the building of King SOLOMON'S temple (about 1000 B.C.) indicates the nature of early trade. The king, designing to build Yahweh a temple, sends messengers to the king of Tyre, the ruler of the energetic little sea-faring Phœnician nation dwelling on the Syrian coast below the mountain range of Lebanon.

> "Now therefore command thou that they hew me cedar trees out of Lebanon; and my servants shall be with thy servants; and unto thee will I give hire for thy servants according to all that thou shalt appoint; for thou knowest that there is not among us any that can skill to hew timber like unto the Sidonians."[2]

To which HIRAM, king of Tyre, replies:

> "I have considered the things which thou sentest to me for: and I will do all thy desire concerning timber of cedar and timber of fir . . . My servants shall bring them down from Lebanon unto the sea: and I will convey them by sea in floats unto the place that thou shalt appoint me, and will cause them to be discharged there, and thou shalt receive them: and thou shalt accomplish my desire, in giving food for my household."[3]

Twenty thousand measures of wheat, and twenty measures of pure oil are bartered in exchange for the cedars. Later, the same record tells, King Solomon

[1]Ex. 22. [2]1st Book of Kings. 5. [3]1st Book of Kings. 5.

built a navy, not for fighting purposes, but to fetch gold from Ophir. His subjects, however, are not seamen, and lack seamanship, so "Hiram sent in the navy his servants, shipmen that had knowledge of the sea, with the servants of Solomon. And they came to Ophir, and fetched from thence gold, four hundred and twenty talents, and brought it to King Solomon."

Those early Phœnicians of the 'coasts of Tyre and Sidon' may be regarded as the first nation of traders. Their timber, and the shellfish from which they obtained royal purple dye, comprised their only natural wealth. They turned to the sea, and developed an overseas barter trade which supplied them with raw materials for the crafts in which they came to excel; they made the Mediterranean their home and Tyre and Sidon their workshops and warehouses. The Phœnician merchants bought the embroideries made in Babylon, the spices and perfumes of Arabia, the Egyptian glass, and traded them in the Mediterranean harbours as far west as the coast of Spain. Like the Greeks, they combined trade with piracy. They founded African *Carthage*, 'the new city.' Behind the fortifications of its two fine harbours rose the luxurious homes of Carthage's merchant pirates, who laid claim to all trade in the western Mediterranean, and seized foreign ships met in those waters. This brought them into conflict with the Greeks during the 5th and 4th centuries B.C., and there was fighting whenever Greek and Carthaginian fleets crossed paths in the sea-way.

The primitive economic system of the Indian Aryan race may be studied in the *Vedas*, the ancient sacred poems and traditions of the Hindoos. Here again we find tribes living as great families, each tribe supporting its people by agriculture and hunting, and maintaining a king leader by voluntary gifts. Those Aryan Indians from whom the Vedas have been handed down by word of mouth through at least 3,000 years lived on the northern plains of India. They wore clothing of sheep's wool woven on hand-looms. Their staple foods were milk, butter, grain and fruit, flesh food being eaten only on ceremonial occasions. They made alcoholic drinks, and the *distiller* of these was an important member of the community—the *soma* plant is named as yielding a juice specially distilled for use at religious festivals. Their women plaited grass mats. They ploughed the land, using a plough with a metal share, drawn by oxen, and reaped their corn with sickles. Their houses were of carved wood. The Rig-Veda frequently refers to the labour of the carpenter, joiner and wheelwright, and it mentions the smith as smelting ore, using the wing of a bird to produce a draught.[1]

Horses were ridden in war and in the chase. Boats were hollowed from tree-trunks, but they appear to have been used only for *crossing* rivers. Trade was by barter, and like the early Romans these Indians measured the values of animals and commodities in terms of what could be exchanged for a cow. Gold ornaments were worn and highly esteemed as gifts and rewards; they were probably also acceptable as a form of payment. *Nishka*, which in the Rig-Veda means a necklet, became later the name of a coin. Another ancient Indian book, the *Satapatha Brahmana*, refers to gold as being immortal, born of fire, the seed of Agni the Sun god, bringing abundant life and offspring to its possessors.

The Chinese, who have occupied since the beginning of recorded history their land between the rivers Hwang-ho and Yangtse-kiang, were never a pastoral people. Their staple food has always been grain. The importance of the grain cultivation was signified by an annual ceremonial sowing, the emperor being the sower.

[1]A. A. Macdonell. *A History of Sanscrit Literature.*

From the time of CONFUCIUS THE SAGE, who lived about the 7th century B.C., until the 19th century of our era, there was little change in the economic life of China. Many a time the Tartar tribes from the plains further north raided the capital and seized the best lands; there were new emperors and new officials, but the majority of the people continued to live their customary toilsome, patient lives. The fertile loess soil yielded its crops without the need for deep ploughing. The village communities were self-supporting, each family having its grain and vegetable patch, its pigs and poultry. Flax was grown, and the silk-worm carefully cultivated, clothing being of linen and silk.

The emperor's tax-gatherers made their rounds, collecting a ninth portion of the village produce for the Son of Heaven. The surplus of crops and home-manufactured goods from each province went to the market town and was there exchanged.

Chinese money, in the early days, seems to have taken many forms. Swords, jewels, tortoise shells, gold and silver objects—all were used, "the chief pre-occupation of the government apparently being to keep the people supplied with a sufficiency of primitive money."[1] Small copper models of swords were later used as *coins*, and also rounded discs of copper. "But then," says a Chinese classic, "roguery and violence began to take precedence of right and justice; greed for the possession of riches replaced modesty and humility in men's minds; large fortunes were made by some callous ones, while others were starving before their eyes."[2]

The earliest of the Chinese sword-shaped coins[3] date from the 8th century B.C. Thereafter undue profit-making and the practice of usury increased, and resulted in the creation of a very rich and a very poor class of people, with a great increase of slavery. The founder of

[1]E. H. Parker, *China*. [2]E. H. Parker.
[3]Specimens in British Museum.

the Han dynasty (206 B.C.—A.D. 221) discouraged traders, and a later emperor, *Wu Ti*, forbade merchants to wear silk or to ride in carriages. Rich citizens were fined, and excessively large fortunes confiscated. This emperor also established officials at the capital city, "to prevent traders and shop-keepers from making huge profits, to take charge of transport and delivery, and to keep the price of commodities steady."[1]

The British Parliament, during the 19th century, often discussed Free Trade versus Protection; and there was a lively difference of public opinion as to which were desirable. The Free Traders thought it better that foreign goods should be admitted to the country through British ports without payment of tariff or duty, thus enabling them to be sold retail at the same price as home products. The Protectionists argued that foreign goods ought to be taxed, thus raising their price to the buyer above that of home products. This question had been considered in China before our ancestors were out of their Stone Age.

In the 6th century B.C. the Chinese government was discouraging the admission of foreign goods to China by the use of customs dues and tariffs.[2] The export of Chinese goods was similarly checked. Chinese crops and manufactures, the argument ran, should benefit Chinese consumers—not be handed to foreigners by traders for profit. Only surplus goods should be sent abroad. As to imported goods, they should be limited to such commodities as the people need. "Do not over-value strange goods," said the Chinese Book of History, "and then foreigners will be only too glad to bring them."

But even under the Han dynasty frontier fairs were held, the Chinese exchanging wood, flax and hemp for the horses, pearls and sables offered by the Tartar tribes. Silk, jade and jewels were also smuggled abroad, these oriental luxuries being in such demand among the

[1] E. H. Parker. [2] See Note.

wealthy of western nations that merchants would risk the very great danger and difficulty accompanying their transport to western Asia in order to sell them.

Slavery, in China, was never the essential basis of society as in Greece and Rome. There was no slave market, wherein men, women and children were sold like animals. Criminals and debtors became slaves, but the condition was regarded as one of misfortune, and was often of a temporary nature.

CHAPTER III

IN GREECE: FREEMEN AND SLAVES

THE people known to us as the ancient Greeks lived on the mainland of Greece and on the adjacent shores and islands of the Mediterranean and Ægean Seas. They first came into history about 1200 B.C. when, as hardy, sea-going tribes, they were beginning to measure their strength against the earlier Minoan folk centred in Crete and the fortress-towns of Mycenæ and Tiryns. Eight centuries later the civilisation of the Greeks—their art, literature, crafts and system of government—was showing finer developments than any civilisation preceding it. This was due, in great part, to the high value which Greek thought placed on the ideal of *freedom*, which included *leisure*.

The early tribes settled, each tribe about the *polis* (fortified place) of its head-man or 'king.' Greece is a country of barren mountain ridges separating deep valleys; the fertile soil is limited; and the Greeks lacked the abundance of real wealth ensured to the Egyptians and Sumerians by the rich alluvial lands and sub-tropical climates of the Nile and Euphrates' deltas. The Greeks had four ways of supplying their material needs; they could hunt in the mountains, cultivate a small quantity of wheat and more olives and grapes in the valleys, fish off the coast, and trade their olive oil to other Mediterranean peoples for corn.

The Dorian Greeks, founders of the city of Sparta, made a virtue of necessity, and taught their children to take pride in the endurance of hunger, exposure and pain. Spartans were even disposed to scorn their fellow-countrymen, the Ionian Greeks, because the latter valued normally, as good and desirable things, the corn, oil, wine and fruit their land produced. A tribe of tough warriors were the Dorian Greeks, strong and sinewy as the shrubs growing on their mountains but, like them, lacking the grace and beauty that comes of culture. While man is using the whole of his energy in combating cold, hunger and adverse conditions he cannot put forth the flowers of the mind—the arts, crafts and creative inventions. The Spartan boy and girl, nurtured on scanty food of the plainest and most monotonous kind, subjected to pain, privation and exposure from early childhood, taught to regard fighting as the end of life, and endurance as its glory, developed hardy, active bodies and muscles like steel, but narrow, unreceptive and unimaginative minds, capable of few ideas.

The early Ionian Greeks cultivated their small farms in valleys opening to the sea. Their houses were simple wooden structures, mere sleeping shelters built round the unroofed courtyard which formed the centre of family life. Furniture was limited to the essential—wooden bench, stone or trestle table, pots for food and water, the housewife's loom. This simplicity of life the Greeks continued to love in their later, wealthier days; it was the basis of the freedom they valued and boasted, a freedom of movement which refused to be impeded by unnecessary possessions—superfluous clothing and household gear, any accumulation of goods which might become a burden, tending to fetter the owner's physical or mental activity.

We should note here that this idealisation of individual freedom, this love of leisure, could only be gratified, *during the ages before the discovery of steam and electric power*, as long as men contented themselves with a life simple and limited in the extreme. The owner of rich land in a favourable climate might, if he were undisturbed by envious neighbours, supply his own needs with minimum of labour, and enjoy much leisure—but his was an exceptional case. The hermit might sustain life on a diet of roots and berries, but such existence was slow starvation, and his ill-nourished brain lost the power of appreciating reality, and presented his mind with fantastic visions. Before the great natural forces of steam and electricity were harnessed to the service of man, there was only one certain way of securing personal leisure—by obliging others to work for you. This fact the Greeks accepted, and with it the institution of slavery. Household slaves play their part in Greek history and drama from its beginning. In the great days of Athens a free citizen who did not own at least one slave was esteemed poor indeed. As Hendrik van Loon says:

> "The Greek city, whenever it was not ruled by a king or a tyrant, was run by and for the freemen, and this would not have been possible without a large army of slaves, who outnumbered the free citizens at the rate of six or five to one. . . . The slaves did all the cooking and baking and candlestick making of the city. They were the tailors and the carpenters and the jewellers and the school-teachers and the book-keepers, and they tended the store and looked after the factory while the master went to the public meeting to discuss questions of war or peace, or visited the theatre to see the latest play. . . ."[1]

The small valley farms, with their corn lands and vineyards and olive groves passed from father to son for many generations; to their labours on the land the owners added boat building, sea-fishing, and trading ventures along the Mediterranean coasts. Centuries passed, the population increased; the *polis* of the chief

[1] *The Story of Mankind.*

grew into a city with market place, town-hall and streets of dwellings, the town houses of the farmers. Each city with its surrounding farm and forest land was known as a *city-state*, ruled, in the case of Athens, by its assembly or town-meeting of all the free citizens.

In the 5th century B.C. the question of food supply became a serious one, for the quantity of corn which could be grown on the little farms did not increase with the population. The people of the city-state of Athens dealt with this problem in three ways, by limiting their families, by encouraging in all possible ways the import of corn, and by making exile a common punishment—law-breakers were shipped away to some foreign coast, there to found a 'colony.' The Athenian father was neither expected nor desired to allow a weakling baby to grow up, nor one he had not the means to support. It was his duty to decide, before the child was five days old, whether he would rear it; if so, it was formally presented to the family, if not, it was taken from the house and exposed in a pot or basket in a public place, where it died, or was rescued and adopted by some childless or wealthier person.

The Athenian farmer and importer of grain were obliged by laws to send their corn to the public granaries of Athens and nowhere else. There it was weighed, and two-thirds of it were dispatched to the city market, where the merchants had to share it—no merchant might buy more than fifty measures. The remaining third was at the disposal of the owner. So essential was the import of foreign corn that citizens were forbidden to lend money to masters of ships unless such vessels were commissioned to bring back a cargo of grain to Athens.[1] So the jars of olive-oil, the pottery and other work of the Greek craftsman went forth, and the grain came in.

The great Greek philosopher ARISTOTLE wrote, in the 4th century B.C.:

[1] Zimmern.

> "As the benefits of commerce were more widely extended by importing commodities of which there was a deficiency and exporting those of which there was an excess, the use of currency became an indispensable device. As the necessaries of Nature were not all easily portable, people agreed, for purposes of barter, mutually to give and receive some article which, while it was itself a commodity, was practically easy to handle in the business of life; some such article as iron or silver, at first defined simply by size and weight, although, finally, they went further and set a stamp on every coin to relieve them from the trouble of weighing it, the stamp impressed upon the coin being an indication of quantity."[1]

The Greeks of Lydia, in Asia Minor, began to use *coins* for money in the 7th century B.C. In the British Museum we may see their coins, small lumps of electrum stamped with the seal of merchant or ruler. Prof. Zimmern says that within a generation of its invention, all the Greek states were coining money, and those citizens to whom debts of various commodities were owing, pressed their debtors to pay coin instead. We shall examine other effects of this invention of coins, in a later chapter.

The 5th and 4th centuries B.C. are often called the *Greek Golden Age*. Why '*golden*,' we may ask. The term is just one of many which point out how widespread became the idea of the unique value of gold. This metal, though not essential to man, and of limited use, tends to be regarded as the symbol of supreme excellence. So the period of Greece's greatest people and finest achievements must be called its Golden Age. Let us consider the economic position of the Athenians at this time.

Athens is no longer a city of farmers and fishers. The

[1](Polit. 1.6. trans. Welldon.)

wealthier citizens have left their farms to the management of slave stewards, or leased them to poorer men. They live in the city, occupying their time with its government, trade and shipping. There is no king; the ruling body is a council of citizens presided over by a member of one of the leading Athenian families. All Athenian freemen have the right to vote when laws are being made or altered. Large numbers of foreign traders and craftsmen now live in Athens; these people were not welcomed, nor are they granted full citizen rights, but since they brought money with them, or some special craft or skill, they are allowed to stay. Money-owners, indeed, are beginning to command the respect formerly paid only to heroes and land-owners, for since the invention of coins all the Mediterranean peoples are becoming ever more fascinated by these symbols of the possession of power and wealth. From the silver mines of Laurion, near Athens, slaves dig the silver from which the Athenian coins are made—the *obols* exchangeable for so many desirable things, from a cargo of corn to a slave's freedom. The richest and most influential citizens of Athens are now those who hold shares in the Laurion mines. The mine-slaves work under conditions so bad that even a strong man is soon worn out—a master can utter no worse threat to a lazy house-slave than that of selling him to the mines.

We have said that even wealthy Greeks maintained simplicity in their personal lives. They did not cumber their bodies with heavy clothing of embroidered cloth, or build themselves pompous, over-furnished dwellings. They had an inherent taste for beauty of form and line, and wanted to see around them objects expressing that beauty. Two essentials of Greek house-keeping were the jar and the pot. Corn, wine and olive-oil, honey, and dried fruits, the staple foods of the Greeks, were all stored in clay vessels; even when broken the pots had a use, being handy for recording memoranda, as we should use scrap-paper. In this Golden Age of Greece there is a great and constant demand for pottery, and the Athenian pottery-making quarter, the *Cerameicos*, is a very busy place. Families of craftsmen vie with each other to produce specimens of greater excellence and beauty, and compete for merchants' orders for both home trade and export. (A fine collection of this pottery to-day awaits our inspection in the British Museum; the painted scenes from Greek life which adorn the jars, vases, cups, plates, etc., give interesting details which would otherwise have been lost to us.)

Above the city, on the hill of the Acropolis, stand the beautiful pillared temples built by the Athenians—the great Parthenon, shrine of the patron goddess Athene, and the smaller shrines. The walls and columns of the temples are of marble, the columns fluted, the frieze above them carved with life-like carvings of men and horses in motion. These buildings, and the statues adorning them, the colossal bronze Athene, thirty feet in height, the ivory and gold Athene, the bronze image of the Wooden Horse of Troy, with more we have not space to name here, represent the thank-offering of the Athenians to the gods for victory against the hosts and fleets of the Great Kings of Persia. Master-masons, free artisans and slaves had all worked together upon the fabric of the temples, receiving for their labour each the same wage, a *drachma* a day.[1]

They were very fine, very impressive, those Greek temples. But the architect of the Greek temple and dwelling omitted to plan for sanitation. No Greek had dreamed of the connexion between the presence of stagnant, dirty water and that of plague. So Athens of the Golden Age was without an adequate water supply—its citizens allowed sewage to lie in pools in the narrow

[1]*Francotte*, quoted by Zimmern in *The Greek Commonwealth*.

streets—and plague helped war to bring the Golden Age to an end.

It is sad to see how often Athenian genius was wronged, and Greek love of freedom betrayed by greed and the desire for profit making. The noble families, supported by the work of others, free to follow considerations of art, literature and politics, so far forgot that they were utterly dependent on the labour of slaves as to regard with contempt citizens occupied with the crafts—even such great artists as the sculptors whose work adorned the temples. It was ignoble, said the aristocrats, for artists to sell their fine works of art for money—and worse to sell them to foreigners. But though the aristocrats thus condemned trade, we do not find that they personally refused to share the profits of the Laurion silver mines. As time went on the two classes of citizens drew apart.

In the beginning, Greek overseas trade and piracy sailed together. The early seafaring adventurer went forth to gain wealth by the cheapest and simplest means—he would trade if he were not strong enough to take by force. The historian Thucydides says that the pioneers of Greek trade in the West were the pirates of Cumæ. . . . Two trading leagues were formed later, for mutual protection against such active foreign trader-pirates as the Phœnicians and Carthaginians. One, the *Eretrian League*, included the ship-owners of Eretria, Miletus, Sybaris and Etruria; the other, the *Chalcidian League*, those of Chalcis, Samos, Corinth and Cumæ (then a Greek colony). The charts of the routes rowed and sailed by their fleets were the earliest maps of the Mediterranean region, and they divide with the Phœnicians the honour of being pioneer explorers of the Adriatic and West Mediterranean seas.

CHAPTER IV

ROME: THE WORLD'S MARKET

NINE centuries, at least, before the time of Christ, primitive tribes living north and south of the river Tiber met for barter at a point where the stream shallowed to fordable depth. The chiefs who held the near hill (afterwards the Hill Palatine) collected tolls from the traders who used the ford. A market grew up. This was the beginning of the city of Rome.

Cattle were exchanged for corn and wine; and an *ox* was the measure by which the price of other animals and goods was fixed. Thus ten sheep might be traded for one ox. Later, we find the Roman farmers buying and selling with large oblong copper coins, each stamped with the image of an ox. But before this time strange ships had sailed up the Tiber, and ruddy-skinned people, the *Etruscans*, had begun to make settlements on the land north of the river. The trade by the ford increased; the Latin folk living on its south side bringing their cattle and corn to the Etruscans in exchange for iron weapons and tools. By 800 B.C. the Etruscan villages had grown into towns, strongly fortified, and Rome also had become a city, walled and gated; this Rome Etruscan warriors captured, and their chief ruled it from his palace on the Hill Palatine. For two and a half centuries his family ruled, until the Latins, then called Romans, rebelled successfully against his last descendant, Tarquin, and drove the Etruscans away. Thereafter, for more than 500 years Rome was governed by a council, the Senate, and two chief officers, the Consuls, chosen by its chief citizens. We mention the Etruscans here because under their rule the plain little city, not much more than a walled camp, where stagnant pools bred fever in the rainy season, was extended, and drained by the building of a great arched sewer, the *Cloaca Maxima*, so massively constructed that it remains to this day.

Like the Greeks, the Romans of Rome's early days lived on the produce of their rather poor farms, and only when they had a *surplus* of some one commodity sought to exchange it for other wanted goods. They were not ship-builders or travellers, but home-keeping folk, suspicious of foreigners. They valued things for use, not for beauty. They guarded jealously their homes and possessions; and were on the lookout to seize an advantage from the tribes whose territory bordered on Latium. Disciplined warriors, as well as hard-working farmers, were the early Romans and their sons; and after the Etruscan kings had been driven out the policy of the Senate was the gradually extended conquest of neighbouring peoples, until the land of Italy was presently ruled from Rome.

We have seen that the Greeks loved simplicity of life and freedom to enjoy leisure; they had no desire for superfluous goods. The Romans liked to possess for the sake of possessing. Especially they realised that the possession of LAND gave them power over both the people the land supported and the crops and raw materials it produced. The lust to possess, the desire to administer, to exercise authority, became the expression of the Roman spirit, and its ultimate outcome was the vast, unwieldy Roman Empire of the first four centuries A.D.

We can make a useful comparison between Greeks and Romans. Both, in their early times, worked small holdings, living mainly on the produce of their labour; both owned few slaves. Both regarded their small city state with an ardent patriotism. As the centuries passed,

Greek and Roman communities each tended to divide into a small rich class and a large poor class, while the number of slaves in both communities increased until they outnumbered the freemen by three or four to one. These similar changes were brought about in the same way, by common causes.

Cause 1. The practice of *Usury*, which is lending goods or money at interest. The unsuccessful or unfortunate land-holder would borrow seed or money from his more fortunate neighbour, agreeing to repay loan and interest in a given time, and pledging a portion of land, a slave, or even one of his children as security.

Borrowing was always easier than repayment, and unless a very good harvest or other luck helped the debtor, he became poorer by the loss of his security when settling time arrived, or he would borrow of a second neighbour, pledging more valuable security, to pay off the first loan. Many a land-owner, having thus postponed from year to year the day when he must face accumulation of debt, saw his farm taken over by his creditor, the wealthier neighbour from whom he had borrowed; he became, at best, a tenant, hiring land once his own. Many a son, inheriting his father's homestead, inherited also a *mortgage*[1] which he could never hope to pay off, and interest charges which took, yearly, all the best produce of the farm. Younger sons of a debtor father were left without patrimony, daughters without dowry, and all belonged, henceforth, to the class of poor citizens obliged to live by the sale of their time and labour. Long before the invention of coins this practice of usury had brought undue wealth of land and goods to the few and poverty to the many; but after their invention a class of professional money-lenders arose who throve on the misfortunes of their borrowers, and made a bad matter worse by establishing a trade in debts. In 6th century Athens we find the wise law-

[1]See Note.

maker Solon decreeing a 'release from burdens,' and including in his code a law forbidding the imprisonment of the debtor. In the 4th century the Roman laws of *Licinius* provided (a) that interest already paid on debts should be deducted from the principal, and (b) that no single citizen should hold more than 500 acres of the common land.

Cause 2. Victory in war was followed by the enslavement of a larger or smaller number of the vanquished. The slave-market of the victorious nation would be glutted with cheap slaves. In Athens this condition followed the Athenian attack upon the island Greeks who withheld tribute; in Rome it was the continued result of Roman conquests throughout the western world. After the destruction of Carthage, the majority of the surviving citizens were shipped as slaves to Rome.

There came a time when the lack of unity among the Greek city-states gave the Roman military power the opportunity of conquering Greece; thereafter Greece was but a province of Rome, and the best art and craftsmanship of the Greeks passed (either by loot or purchase) into the hands of super-wealthy Romans. It was this class of the Roman people which chiefly benefited by the conquests which continually enlarged the Roman Empire. The historian Mommsen says:

> "The money dealings throughout the range of the Roman state were monopolised by the Romans. . . . The unscrupulous employment of Rome's political ascendancy, for the benefit of the private interests of every wealthy Roman, rendered a usurious system of interest universal, as is shown by the treatment of the war-tax imposed by Sulla on the province of Asia in 670, which the Roman capitalists advanced; it swelled with paid and unpaid interest within 14 years to six-fold its original amount. The communities had to sell their public buildings, works of art, and

jewels; parents had to sell their grown-up children to meet the claims of the Roman creditor. It was no rare occurrence for the debtor to be placed on the rack."[1]

We shall now notice how the business of the production and distribution of goods was carried on within the Roman Empire at the time of its widest extent, when it stretched from Germany to North Africa, from the coasts of France and Spain to the Carpathians, and included Asia Minor, Syria, and Britain.

Italy, centre of the Empire, was an agricultural country, producing corn, wine, olive-oil, vegetables and dairy produce. The majority of the farms were owned by landlords who never, in the course of their lives, did a day's farming, but employed slave stewards to superintend the work of slave labourers and to market the crops and animals. The great city of Rome needed more corn than the Italian fields could provide, but wine and oil were exported to Egypt and other Mediterranean countries from the ports of Ostia and Puteoli. Italy's imports, however, were far greater than her exports. A third of Rome's corn came from Egypt, and more from the province of North Africa. The manufacturing city of Alexandria sent linen, paper, glass and embroideries, and also forwarded from the far East silks, spices, pearls and precious stones. Greek ships brought marble, purple dye obtained from shell fish, honey, pottery and wines; fleets from Africa marble, ivory, sponges, gold-dust, wild beasts for the popular shows, and negro slaves. Building materials and metals, especially gold and iron, were imported from the Baltic provinces, woollen clothing and pottery came from Gaul, copper from Spain, lead and oysters from Britain.

All these commodities poured into Rome, which was a huge market town—the greatest the world had seen.

[1] *History of Rome.*

People who bought in Rome might purchase the finest goods the world of the period could produce, in variety such as never before had been gathered in one place; and buyers could have their purchases readily taken by way of the excellent Roman roads, or by regular trade routes by sea, to any other city of the Empire. Who then, came to buy in Rome?

Only a small percentage of the Empire's population. The masses of the people were slaves or impoverished persons. MONEY, without which the goods could not be bought, was nearly all in the hands of relatively few people.

From 335 B.C. Roman citizens had used coins of bronze and silver, issued from mints at Capua and Rome. Gold coins were first issued in 217 B.C. The supreme right of coining money was at first held by the Senate, and became later the prerogative of the Roman emperors. Had the emperors been obliged to *buy* the metals for the mints little profit might have accrued to them from their right of issue; but much metal came from tributary lands as tribute or tax. Moreover the coins were not always made of pure metal—an alloy was used. The mints were therefore a source of wealth to the emperors, and the new coins went into the imperial treasury to issue forth as payment for goods and services supplied (other than by tribute or slave labour) to the imperial household.

The greater Roman emperors were fabulously wealthy; it was in their power to dispose of, or assign to others, immense stores of goods and commodities over and above the maximum they could personally use or enjoy. Some were successful generals, enriched by the spoils of war; some inherited their wealth. After the emperors came, in order of riches, the money-lenders, the governors of the Roman provinces, army officers in high command, and the official class generally. Each conquered province was ruled by a Roman governor, whose appointment was generally for a year. The governors had power to tax the people, and used the power to their own advantage; they would sell to the highest bidder the office of tax-gatherer, and the official appointed repaid himself with interest from the excessive sums demanded of the citizens. The hatred felt for the 'publican' (tax-gatherer) is indicated in the gospels.[1]

Luxury and squalor met in Rome and the other cities of the Empire. The houses of the wealthy were huge, pretentious brick buildings, wherein the owners collected, according to the measure of their wealth, carpets from Egypt, silk hangings from China, fur rugs from the German forests, the fine, slender pottery and furniture of the Greek craftsman; rare statuary by famed Greek sculptors, heavily jewelled caskets of Eastern origin. In Dalmatia at the present day, a whole town is built within the area formerly enclosed by the palace walls of the Roman emperor Diocletian. This enormous building was certainly exceptional in size; but a house requiring a domestic staff of at least a hundred slaves was the ordinary establishment of a moderately wealthy Roman official. The meals prepared in such houses were frequently elaborate banquets lasting several hours and comprising a great variety of courses, delicacies being imported from all parts of the Empire.

The clothing worn was as rich and varied as the food eaten. Apart from the ceremonial garb of the priest, the senator and the civil officer, or the uniform of the soldier, fashions changed in Rome much as they do in the western world of fashion now, and clothes were accumulated as well as other commodities. . . . The other side of Roman life displayed a great population of citizens not merely poor as the Athenian potter or stonemason had been poor, but without craft, trade, work or self-respect; half starved, in rags, existing in dreadful slums; paupers, debtors and their children, having

[1]Matt., 9. Luke, 19.

nothing to lose but their lives, ready to commit crimes for payment. To these victims of an economic system based on slavery and usury the emperors flung loaves of bread on festival days.

Thus, throughout the Roman Empire the military, official and money-lending and dealing classes gained nearly all the available money, and with it bought and accumulated the Empire's real wealth, wasting what they could not consume. In consequence of which the producers of the wealth lived in poverty or sank into slavery. Thousands of slaves indeed lived luxuriously in the palaces of their masters—but they were without the power to purchase in their own right as men and women even a penny loaf in the rich market of Rome.

CHAPTER V

FROM THE DARK AGES: FEUDALISM

BEYOND the confines of the Roman Empire lived the unconquered peoples; the primitive tribes of Nordic folk in Germany and Scandinavia; the Mongols north and east of the Caucasus and the Caspian Sea. By gradual inroads, by sudden thrusts, by intermittent attacks extending over a period of five centuries, these pushed southward, and the tax-ridden, poverty-rotten civilisation of Rome gave way before them. Within the Empire itself there was civil war from time to time—the commanders of the various groups of legions vying for supremacy and the throne of the emperor. The evil state of things continued—money-lenders and officials snatching for wealth and authority, the middle class families becoming richer or poorer, the poor sinking to slavery, the slave class still increasing.

Roman cities, ill-defended by indifferent or unpaid legionaries, admitted the invaders, with whom the citizens made peace. The officials and money-lenders fled, leaving their palaces to barbarian chiefs who had no use for the accumulation of wealth, the statues, bronzes, mosaics, Greek vases, Persian carpets, Chinese silks; the slave chefs with their huge kitchen equipment and thousand delicacies for the banquet; the masseuses and perfumers; the gardeners with their craft of beauty. The barbarian chiefs were disposed to roast half an ox on the banqueting-room floor, never minding if the palace burnt with it, and to carve their joints with their daggers. Only gold coins and objects, and brightly coloured clothing they sought and valued.

Grass, brushwood, finally trees, grew over the Roman roads that had linked the cities. Agricultural land went back to the wild; creeping plants wreathed the ruined walls of the palaces. Buying and selling in large markets ceased. Men lived as and how they might—neighbour bartering with neighbour his spare commodity, or exchanging skill for skill. But for the monks, many a craft and agricultural secret might have been forgotten. Well that here and there a monastery remained, its inhabitants carrying on continuously the routine of study and work prescribed by its founder! Within the precincts of the monasteries were preserved to later generations the traditions of Roman Law, Greek philosophy, and the Christian religion (which had been adopted by the Roman State in the 4th century A.D.), together with a knowledge of various arts and crafts.

. . . .

Such was the condition of things in Europe when, in the 7th century A.D., a new Arab empire arose, founded by MUHAMMAD the Prophet of Mecca, and established by his successors, the Caliphs of Baghdad and Cordova. This Muhammadan Empire comprised the lands conquered by the Caliphs' armies, and included all peoples adopting the Muhammadan religion. By the 9th century it embraced Arabia, Egypt, Persia, north Africa, Syria and Spain.

Baghdad, the city of the Caliphs, was the greatest market of the world in this 9th century. Tribute and merchandise flowed into it as formerly into Rome. *Cordova*, in Spain, also became a Caliph's capital; and here rose the Moorish architecture typified to-day by its great Mosque and by the palace of the Alhambra in Granada. The Caliphs' officers restored the Roman roads, built new ones, constructed aqueducts and bridges. Trade with the far East was revived, and products of China, India and the interior of Russia might be purchased in the market booths of Baghdad. Textiles, glass and pottery, metal work, fine leather goods, and paper, were among the manufactured articles sold.

In its earlier days, Muhammadan rule was marked by a simplicity and honesty that commended it to the people of Asia Minor and Syria, who had suffered much from the extortions of Roman tax-gatherers. According to Muhammad's laws, as set forth in his book *Al Koran*, the war leader or prince took one-fifth of the spoils of war, the rest being shared among his followers. The earlier Caliphs lived simple and strenuous lives, disdaining to impress their subjects by display of luxury. The later ones, however, gradually assumed the pomp and arrogance of Oriental princes surrounded from childhood by slaves, growing to depend utterly upon the unpaid and unrecognised labour of those they despised as inferiors, and regarding the people they ruled merely as sources of tribute—producers and purveyors of the commodities and luxuries demanded by the Court. And the trade of Baghdad, like that of Rome, benefited the officials and wealthy merchants much more than the whole people of the Empire. In one respect only the trading system of the Arab was to be preferred to that of the Roman. *Al Koran*, the book which Muhammadans believed to contain Allah's precise commands as delivered to the Prophet, forbade usury, and threatened the merchant who lent money at interest with punishment hereafter:

> "They who devour usury shall not arise from the dead but as he ariseth whom Satan hath infected by a touch; this shall happen to them because they say: Truly, selling is but usury—and yet God hath permitted selling and forbidden usury. He therefore who . . . . abstaineth from usury shall have what is past forgiven him, and his affair belongeth unto God.

But whosoever returneth to usury shall be the companions of hell fire."[1]

The extortions of the money-lender were therefore, if not prevented, at least discouraged by Arab religion.

The *Franks* (axemen) occupied the Roman province of Gaul (now France) and intermarried with the settled population which had been bred to Roman civilisation. The Frank kings, wishing to placate the Roman deity, accepted the form of the Christian religion. One of these kings, KARL MARTEL, led his warriors against a Muhammadan force that was advancing from Spain, and defeated it. This stand against the Muhammadans was the beginning of the Frank rise to power in Europe. The grandson of Karl Martel was *Karl the Great* or CHARLEMAGNE, the hero of French romance, who in the early 9th century ruled over an empire stretching from Brittany to the Upper Danube, and from the Lower Rhine to Rome.

But Rome was no longer a world market. To Europeans of Charlemagne's day it was just the Pope's city—the religious centre of Christendom. Nor was *Aachen*, the Frank emperor's capital, a city of outstanding trade. For this was a period when each land-owner, holding his land nominally by the king's favour, but actually by right of his own power to keep it, lived on its produce, employing the labour of his tenants and serfs. There was hunting in the forest, fishing in the river, the cultivation, in rough fashion, of the fertile acres, and pasturing of sheep, cattle and goats. It was again a time of local barter, not of buying and selling. Trade and transport—the whole commercial system known to the Roman Empire of earlier days, had broken down. Instead of a united Europe, town linked to town, market to market, with merchants and merchandise passing freely along

[1]*Al Koran*, Chap. II, trans., Sale.

good main roads, this Europe of the 7th to the 11th centuries was divided, parcelled out into hundreds of small territories, each the domain of a baron whose word was law to his dependents.

> "When the Empire's defences broke down, when the king's law failed to operate, the landless man and the small farmer found themselves a prey to grasping baron and marauding Viking, and saved themselves in the only possible way—by seeking the protection of the strongest local lord, to whom they pledged themselves in service."[1]

Thereafter developed the economic system known as *feudalism*—*feudum* meaning land held in virtue of service rendered. The feudal system of society grew up. In theory the king was the owner of the whole land, his nobles receiving from him their holdings in return for homage and the maintenance of armed companies ready to serve and support him. The baron pledged himself to lead his company to fight in the king's wars, if so desired, for a given number of days each year. The knight became the baron's tenant on similar terms; the *villein* or the freeman paid for his farm in service to the knight; the artisans of the baron's town or village plied their crafts under his protection, his requirements being their first consideration. Because there was no general assurance of peace and security—no supreme Dictator to whom all *must* submit, nor common code of law and order to which all might agree to submit for the common good—every Producer was obliged to buy safety from one of the non-producing fighting land-holders who made warfare their profession and life interest.

Let us look at a single feudal domain, the size, perhaps, of one of the largest English counties. It has up-

[1] *A Book of Modern Peoples.*

lands where sheep feed, a tract of forest, cornlands, and pasture. The castle of the baron, his residence, court and garrison in one, is built of great blocks of stone, set in commanding position, possibly on a bluff above the river. Adjacent to it is his town, the home of the artisans on whose crafts the baron depends—armourers, wheelwrights, saddlers, masons, perhaps weavers—although the greater part of the spinning and weaving is done in the farm-houses. Dotted about the domain are the 'halls' of the knights, timbered dwellings of good size, each having a large main room built of logs, with earthen, rush-strewn floor, and perhaps an upper storey or extension providing rooms for the lady of the house, her daughters and maids. Adjacent are the dairy and kitchen, barns and outhouses. The villeins have yet simpler wooden dwellings, while the *cottars* sleep in huts of wattle and clay. The labour of the villeins and cottars, men, women and children, begins with the dawn and lasts till sunset. They are regarded as belonging to the estate on which they were born; they change masters when the land changes hands; but they are not bought or sold in open market.

The villeins and cottars are the food producers. With spades, with primitive wooden plough-shares and harrows they prepare the soil for the seed, which they broadcast and then leave to God. Bird-robbers, indeed, the boys attack with stones, but the much more destructive insect-pests go unregarded. With scythe and sickle they reap at harvest—every available hand helping—for on safe harvesting depends the fortune of winter, whether sufficiency or scarcity. There is sheep-shearing in June, with the wool to wash, and later to card and spin; the farmer's wife, daughters and serf-women are always busy. Cheese must be pressed, butter churned, and there is a great slaughtering of beasts, and curing and salting of meat in the autumn, for lacking root crops, which are not grown, fodder runs short in the winter.

To the halls and barns of baron and knights go the best of the meat, poultry, cheese, butter, corn, flour, wool and hides. Next come the shares of the villein farmers. The cottars are lucky if coarse bread and hard cheese do not fail them the year through, and if autumn brings a plenty of nuts, berries and apples. Ale they may drink, but meat is festive fare.

Garments are of wool, linen and leather. A *new* garment is regarded, by all classes except the nobility, as an expensive luxury, only to be indulged in on such a special occasion as a wedding-day. Thick woollen cloth and homespun, coarse linen, will last more than a single lifetime, and clothing is bequeathed by will from parents to children. A leathern jerkin, with a sheep-skin or goat-skin belted over it in severe weather, is the labourer's wear.

If the harvest fails, if epidemic sickness (prevalent, and due to the absence of drainage or sanitation) devastates the domain, the community endures starvation to a greater or lesser degree. Or, should a quarrel break out between the baron and his neighbour of the adjoining territory, every able-bodied man must leave work for war—and again poverty, and perhaps famine, will threaten, since the cattle and crops are then subject to the enemy's raids.

Roads were but ill-defined tracks, and muddy narrow lanes where the pack-mule picked his way over deep hollows of dried mud in the summer, and floundered in boggy soil at other seasons. No one left home unless he were compelled by the call to arms, by urgent business, or by the demands of his religion. The last-named imposed pilgrimage to the burying-place of a saint or martyr as a penance for sin; and as the Middle Ages advanced such pilgrimages became very popular. At the shrines of the saints buying and selling began again, and the institution of *fairs* resulted. As the time of the saint's feast day approached pedlars would gather at the shrine to sell food and relics to the expected pilgrims. The local overlord of the place, its bishop or baron, found it profitable to hire out sites for stalls and booths to these pedlars; by degrees a considerable trade in miscellaneous goods developed, and presently the saint's fair became the recognised annual market of the neighbourhood. The Fair of St. Denys, at Paris, instituted in the 7th century, was the earliest of these medieval fairs.

CHAPTER VI

SIX CENTURIES OF AGRICULTURE

IN this and the two succeeding chapters we shall consider more particularly the lives of the people of England between A.D. 1100 and 1700.

The England of 1100 was a more thickly wooded country than ours, having more common and forest, its arable land worked in long strips, undivided by hedges. The titular owners of the land were the barons and bishops who had supported the Norman king WILLIAM I at the battle of Hastings; it was shared among them after the defeat of Saxon Harold and his earls. Some land also belonged to the Church; the area held in the name of abbeys and monasteries tended to increase. Each holding was similar to that described in the previous chapter, with more or less of woodland, common and arable according to the locality.

About a third of the arable land was cultivated for the barons and knights by their tenants. The rest was shared by the tenants (villeins and cottars) in proportion to their status. Each year a portion equal to a third of the whole was left fallow, the weeds, when ploughed in, forming a natural manure. The heavy wooden ploughs were drawn by oxen, generally eight to a team. The seed was broadcast. The yield of corn, compared with the standard expected to-day was very poor. Writing in the 13th century WALTER OF HENLEY, a monk interested in farming, cites six bushels to the acre as being an average crop—twenty-five bushels would not be regarded as a fair average crop now. Clover was not grown, and grass hay the sole winter feed for cattle and horses. Pigs, poultry and geese were kept; the pigs, in charge of the village swine-herd, rooting in the woods, the geese and poultry feeding on the common or waste land. The meadow or hay land was fenced in from early spring to hay harvest; later in the year it pastured sheep and cattle.

The best farming of the Middle Ages was done on the lands belonging to the abbeys and monasteries. These were very extensive. Many a robber baron, unrighteous bishop or feckless knight, persuaded when they came to die that their lives had been evil, left by will a portion of their holding to the local monastery in payment for the prayers of the monks. The religious orders of the Benedictines and Cistercians devoted much time to farming; and their exemption from war service gave them the advantage over the lay cultivators. The annual round of regular work on the abbey lands was seldom disturbed; the brothers dug and planted, directed the labours of their serfs, experimented and recorded the result of their observations. Well-stocked barns were a feature of a prosperous abbey, and much corn was locally sold. Most famous of these farmer-monks was the order of the Cistercians, whose monasteries numbered a hundred in England alone, and were scattered over Europe. The Cistercians bred fine horses and produced the best of 13th century English wool. On their lands much labour was done by lay monks, poor freemen recruited to the Order as agricultural workers, living within the community and subject to its discipline.

In all ages preceding the discovery of solar energy and electric power—that is, while food could only be secured by human and animal labour, the *majority* of persons in any community were obliged to work. We have seen how the small leisured class of Greek citizens was dependent upon the work of its slaves, and how in the Roman state the same conditions were repeated. In 12th century England, with a population of about 2,000,000, at least two-thirds of the people belonged to the villein class, and if to these we add the cottars, who numbered 90,000 a century earlier, when the Domesday record was made, we realise how few in comparison were the non-producing class, the clergy and nobles.

The villein's holding might be thirty acres. In addition to working his own farm, he was expected to labour three days a week on his lord's land, using his oxen; and certain other dues of work and produce were required of him. The English villeins of the 11th and 12th centuries accepted their position in the feudal system of society. The power of their lords secured their land to them, and protection from interference. It seemed a not unfair bargain that they should labour for the lord when called upon—so long as his demand did not exceed what was customary. But villeins of the 14th century were differently situated. They were less in need of their lord's protection—the supremacy of the king had been fully established in the country. Thrifty villeins, who had sold surplus crops and saved money, approached their lords, offering payment of annual rent instead of payment in labour and war service; the barons and knights were sometimes glad to accept the money—they needed it to spend abroad. A deed or agreement was drawn up in each case, and a copy of this was kept by the villein—henceforth a 'copyholder,' free to devote the whole of his time to his own farm.

In the 14th century land-holders began to cut down their corn-growing land to the minimum required for local use, and to turn their arable land into pasture for sheep. There were two reasons for this: Firstly, the barons and knights who had taken part in the Crusades had sighted the wealth of the East—the silks, the finely dressed leathers, the swords of tempered steel—a great variety of desirable commodities hitherto unknown to them. These foreign goods could only be bought with *money*. Again, the baron who took his company crusading was bound to provide them with food and transport while abroad; the Italian and Venetian purveyors of the ports would demand no low payment for such services. Wanting *money*, what could the land-holder *sell*? Flanders (now Belgium and north-east France) was at that time the centre of the European wool-weaving industry—the Flemish weavers were noted for their excellent cloth. They wanted more wool than their country could produce, and were ready to buy the wool of English sheep, which was of fine quality. Land-holders who kept sheep could sell the wool to English merchants for export to Flanders. Moreover, it suited the baron whose villeins were wanting to pay him money rents instead of labour rents, to turn his arable land into pasture; the sheep needed only a few shepherds to tend them, whereas many labourers were required for ploughing, harrowing, sowing and harvesting. This was the beginning, in our country, of production for *sale abroad* rather than production for *use at home*.

In the year 1348 an epidemic of plague swept through Europe and raged in England. Many thousands of people died, both in the towns and in the villages. After the plague, every land-holder was short of labourers: this was a further reason for increasing the sheep pastures and reducing the arable land. But it was essential that enough corn be grown to provide the manors and towns with bread. Land-holders found it necessary to pay their tenants for their labour, either in privileges or money. Baron A's steward, going to collect his men for the ploughing, would find them gone to work for Baron B., whose steward had bribed them to leave their own village. Serfs whose forefathers had for centuries lived, laboured and died on the manor began to sense freedom and to desire the use of money.

> "*When Adam delved and Eve span,*
> *Who was then the gentleman?*"

ran a rhyme of the period. The land-owners who sat in Parliament passed *Statutes of Labourers* attempting to bind serfs again to the parish within which they were born, and to limit them to the old conditions of work and pay. The Peasants' Rebellion of 1381 was the ultimate result of these statutes. The rebellion was a brave gesture, but its advantage to the peasants was only temporary—they were too ignorant and credulous to hold their own against the better informed land-holders.

Wool went on displacing corn. We find that in 1488 the corn-growing lands had so dwindled that king and parliament passed statutes to encourage tillage. But the large sheep farms were so profitable to their owners that the latter preferred to keep them and buy foreign corn for their own use. They were making fortunes by producing wool for export, while for the artisans and labourers food was scarce and dear. It is recorded by a 15th century chronicler that there was a "mighty army of begging poor," who tramped from monastery to monastery—for the religious houses fed the beggar and gave him a night's lodging.

The feudal system of land tenure died out in England after the Wars of the Roses. From this time onward money was in more general use. Land, labour and commodities—all were bought and sold for money. Land-owners were now of three classes—the gentry, who rented their lands to farmers and lived on the income thus obtained; the yeomen, owners of farms who worked the lands they owned and sold the produce; and small-holders or crofters who, by continuous toil, wrung a hard living out of their tiny holdings. The gentry and larger farmers hired landless men and women to work for them, paying as little for labour as possible because, since they were producing crops for *sale* instead of for immediate use, the making of *profit* was their first concern. The profit was just the difference between the money paid out for rent, seeds, labour, etc. in the course of a year's production, and the money gained by sale of the crops. The richest farmers were those whose production cost them least and who could sell corn, beasts and dairy produce at a high price. The poorest were the small-holders.

In Flanders turnips and clover were grown as field crops from the 16th century onwards; and in the 17th and 18th centuries their cultivation spread through Britain. It ensured feed for cattle the whole year, and also improved the soil; while the general health of the nation benefited by the substitution of fresh meat for the salt (and often half-putrid) joints which had formerly been the inevitable winter diet.

The best English farming of the 16th and 17th centuries was done by the yeomen—the working owners of well-stocked, good-sized farms. Their sons worked beside them in the fields, and they hired labourers according to need at the annual local hiring-fair. Tenant-farmers and small-holders, whose expenses, in proportion to the crops they could sell, were higher, worked incessantly with poorer results. The labourers, hired for the year or season at rates varying from 5d. to 1s. 8d. per day, lived in greater or lesser poverty; its degree depending upon the charitable (or indifferent) attitude of the master and his family, and the heavier or lighter taxes imposed by the government of the period.

The Tudor monarchs, and especially Queen ELIZABETH, realised that the country's food supply was more important than the foreign trade in wool. The population of the towns, and that of London especially, was increasing; and the townspeople, who could not grow corn for themselves but were obliged to buy it from farmers, must be fed. Also there were thousands of landless, workless, half-starved families wandering about; these vagrants were worse off than ever since King HENRY VIII had closed the abbeys and monasteries. They were feared and detested by the more fortunate classes, and particularly by the hard-worked, settled poor people. It is true that they often stole food and clothing—but how else could they live? If they begged they were liable to be publicly whipped or put in the stocks. Some of them, at least, might earn a labourer's wage if pastures were ploughed up and turned into corn land once more!

Laws were made limiting to 2,000 the number of sheep a land-holder might own, ordering the re-building of farm premises, making all able-bodied unemployed men liable to serve as agricultural labourers. Fines were imposed for converting arable land to pasture. Gradually the sheep-runs were reduced, and wheat ripened again on English hillsides. There was more food, but less freedom. In order that land-holders should submit to these laws the government fixed a minimum price for corn, below which price it might not be sold—this limited the quantity of bread the poor could buy; the labourer's wage was also fixed at a low figure, which he was obliged to accept on pain of imprisonment. The sons of labourers were also to be labourers; they were forbidden to become apprenticed to a craft or trade. In Tudor England, as in ancient Greece and Rome, a small leisured class enjoyed wealth and freedom only at the expense of the over-worked, economically unfree majority.

The 17th century saw the beginning of improvements in agricultural methods that resulted, later on, in a much higher yield per acre of the crops grown. An experimenter named JETHRO TULL discovered that, by sowing seed in rows with spaces between them, and frequently hoeing to keep the spaces clear of weeds, and to let air and rain penetrate to the roots of the plants, he could raise heavier crops than his neighbours. Tull also invented a small machine drill for sowing seed evenly. The ancient way of broadcasting seed and letting weeds grow till harvest had been very wasteful. Another great economy was effected when LORD TOWNSHEND (18th cent.) showed that there was no need to leave fields lying fallow every third year; by arranging a rotation of crops—wheat, turnips, barley, clover—the land might be kept in use all the time.

For purposes of comparison we will end this chapter with a glance at 17th century agricultural conditions in Russia and Germany. How was food produced in these two countries, and was it more evenly distributed than in England?

German village life in the Middle Ages had been in many ways similar to that upon an English manor. The arable land had been worked in strips, and the peasants' share divided among them sometimes by lot, sometimes by a permanent assignment to each family, of portions of good and poor land. Ploughing was done in common by the heavy ox-ploughs, each man bringing his two oxen to help make up the teams of eight. Harvesting was also communal work. The services due from peasantry to landlords was fixed by long-standing local customs, existing rather in the memories of the people than in phrase or document. The first consideration of agriculture was the provision of food for the community. This was the state of things down to the end of the 15th century.

Then came a change. The German princes adopted the old Roman code of laws relating to property—the code known by the name of the Emperor JUSTINIAN. In the law-courts of all the German States lawyers argued, and judges pronounced, according to the definitions of this code, which disregarded local custom, and made it possible for the landlords to deny the rights and curtail the freedom of the peasantry. The outcome was a great rising of the peasants against their lords—a revolt which was crushed by the paid soldiers of the nobility. Afterwards, the majority of the villagers, who had been formerly free except in respect of the dues and services rendered for their holdings, were reduced to a more or less degree of servile dependence upon the will of the land-owners. The ownership of the land, and the disposal and distribution of all it produced, passed into the hands of the few.

In Russia this condition of things was even worse. From the time of PETER THE GREAT (1672-1725) until the middle of the 19th century, the food-producers of the country were serfs, bound helplessly to the land and the will of an owning class of fighters or leisured aristocrats.

CHAPTER VII

SIX CENTURIES OF MANUFACTURE

WINDMILLS were used as early as the 12th century. Each manor had its windmill, for which the miller paid rent in service. All the corn of the community was brought to the mill for grinding, the villeins and cottars generally paying the miller in eggs, poultry, etc. Windmills were also built on Church lands; sometimes we find baron or abbot forbidding tenants to build them; they must have their corn ground at *his* mill, and pay his charges. This *monopoly*[1] of the milling industry was very profitable.

The professional baker and brewer appear first as townsmen of the medieval town, working primarily, perhaps, for the baron or bishop, its overlord. The towns were more or less independent—the more independent of them held charters of freedom, and were ruled by the mayor and corporation appointed by their own burgesses. One of the most urgent duties of the medieval mayor and aldermen was to enforce the local regulations controlling the production and sale of bread. Shortage of food, and particularly of bread, was so common a condition that the burgesses lived in continual fear of it. It was the business of the king's justices of the peace in each county to fix "after the feast of St. Michael in each year" the *weight* of the standard loaf to be offered for sale at a penny during the succeeding twelve months. This was done after the local harvest, when the civil officers had made an estimate of the corn

[1]See Note.

available for the period; the ceremony, called the *Assize of Bread*, was a public one. And nothing more surely aroused the wrath of the burgesses than an attempt on the part of a baker to sell short weight loaves, or the sight of mayor and aldermen who failed to punish such dishonest action. The king might be above the law, but the mayor certainly was not. In the records of Coventry (1387) it is stated that "the common people rose and threw loaves at the mayor's head because the bakers kept not the Assaye, neither did the mayor punish them according to his office." There was also an *Assize of Ale*. Ale, made from the malt of barley, was everyone's drink. The wealthy landowner might import a little wine from France for his own and his guests' use, but it was not sold generally.

The people of the manors produced their own cloth and leather. Cottars' and farmers' wives spun woollen and linen thread with the whorl, and later (from 15th century) with the spinning-wheel. Here and there a family would gain a local reputation for the excellence of its work at spindle or loom and earn special money or privileges by working for the castle or monastery. Sometimes the home of such a family would become a centre of its craft, and the master, with his children and apprentices, devote the whole of their working time to producing cloth for exchange or sale. In that case the family had no use for a holding of land, but would live in a town, to be near the market-place. Since it was not producing its own food, in order to live it must both *sell and buy*. Once established, the craft might be passed down from father to son, from mother to daughter for many generations.

There was great variety of handicraft workers during the Middle Ages. Nobody was encouraged to be 'Jack of all trades and master of none.' The artisan's fellow-townsmen expected him to do *one* thing, and to do it well. The burgess could not, for instance, engage a workman who could lay the floors of his new house and might also fit in the window-panes.[1] Carpenter and glazier must each perform his separate function. The cobbler would mend your shoes, but if you needed a new pair you sought the cordwainer. The construction of any large building, such as cathedral or palace, brought together thousands of craftsmen, sometimes of several nationalities.

The medieval craftsman had a much more intensive interest in his craft than the majority of workers to-day. Generally it came to him by inheritance, and his childhood had been spent among those practising it. If he did not learn it in his own home he served from four to seven years (or even longer) as apprentice in the house of a craft master. When fully qualified he became a member of his craft's Gild—his town's association of similar workers. His whole life's interest, as that of his companions, was bound up with this one occupation. And, as a rule, he was profoundly ignorant of everything outside it.

In medieval towns the several industries had their special quarters, named after the occupations carried on —Tanners' Row, Bread Street, Weavers' Alley, etc. Public opinion demanded that workshops should be open to neighbourly inspection—any secret proceedings awakened immediate suspicion.

The 13th and 14th centuries saw the rise and growth of the Craft Gilds. A Craft Gild was the association of all the town's workers in a particular industry for the protection and furtherance of the industry and the mutual benefit of those engaged in it. At first the leading burgesses of the towns were inclined to oppose the formation of these unions, but we find that eventually they were recognised both by the Church and by the municipal authorities as a useful and valuable feature of town organisation. Each Gild was controlled by its

[1]But glass panes were a rare luxury in the Middle Ages.

Warden and Council, who were respected masters of their craft and on festival days wore gorgeous robes and jewelled chains of office. They supervised the work done and helped to maintain its quality, rewarding excellence and condemning shoddiness. They settled terms and conditions of apprenticeship, and also disputes between master and apprentice. They examined the 'masterpiece' of the journeyman[1] who, having ended the term of his apprenticeship and that of his probationary service as paid assistant worker, applied for recognition as master, and the right to practise the craft independently. They disbursed money from the Gild funds to widows of members, and assisted orphans. A craftsman newly come to the town would not be permitted to seek employment or to sell his work until he had been approved by the Gild concerned and admitted to its membership. Thereafter he would regularly pay his subscription in common with the other members—possibly a higher subscription than they, because he was alien to the town.

These manufacturers of the early Middle Ages worked, as a rule, for their masters, friends and neighbours, selling finished commodities and articles in the local market. Woollen cloth was the staple clothing material, and the weaving of woollen cloth was therefore the chief textile industry. Before the time of the Plantagenet king EDWARD III, royalty and nobility had worn fine cloth made in Flanders; but this king aimed at so improving the quality of English weaving that the import of Flanders cloth would be unnecessary. His law of 1337 forbade both the selling of English wool to the Flemings and the buying of foreign cloth for English fairs and markets; he also granted special privileges to Flemish weavers of good repute who would settle in England and teach the craft. Many Flemish weavers did so, for those were troubled days in Flanders; and

[1]See Note.

they found no lack of English apprentices. The king's action turned East Anglia into a weaving area, with cloth-making processes being carried on in all its villages, and with the London and Ipswich merchants' factors buying up much of the cloth to sell in Flanders.

Each length of cloth represented the labour of many workers. The wool, shorn from the sheep, was washed, 'parted' coarse from fine, dyed, softened with oil, and 'carded.' The 'carder' separated knots and drew out impurities, using a wire comb; the *knee-carder* combed it a second time—then it was ready for spinning. Before the invention of the spinning-wheel this operation took the time of a large proportion of the community—*all* girls and unmarried women were expected to employ their leisure time with the spindle—hence the word *spinster* is still used to designate an unmarried woman. The weaver received the skeins and wove the cloth on his hand-loom, the finished length was rid of lumps and loose end by the *burler*. The *fuller* or *walker* washed, beat and stretched the cloth; the *rower* raised the nap by whipping it with teazles; the *shearman* cut the nap even and smooth. Finally the *drawer* went over it with needle and thread, carefully strengthening weak spots.

Each of these artisans made a whole or partial living by his work. The carder or dyer who bought wool from the farmer would sell it to the next craftsman at a price increased by the amount his Gild declared was due to him for his work upon it. The other craftsmen would do the same. And the price for which the finished fabric was offered for sale represented the original cost of the wool plus the cost of each worker's time and labour.

But from the 14th century onward certain sharp-witted craftsmen who had saved money began to change this system of manufacturing cloth. They bought looms, and large quantities of wool, and shared the wool among carders and spinners to whom they paid a wage. The

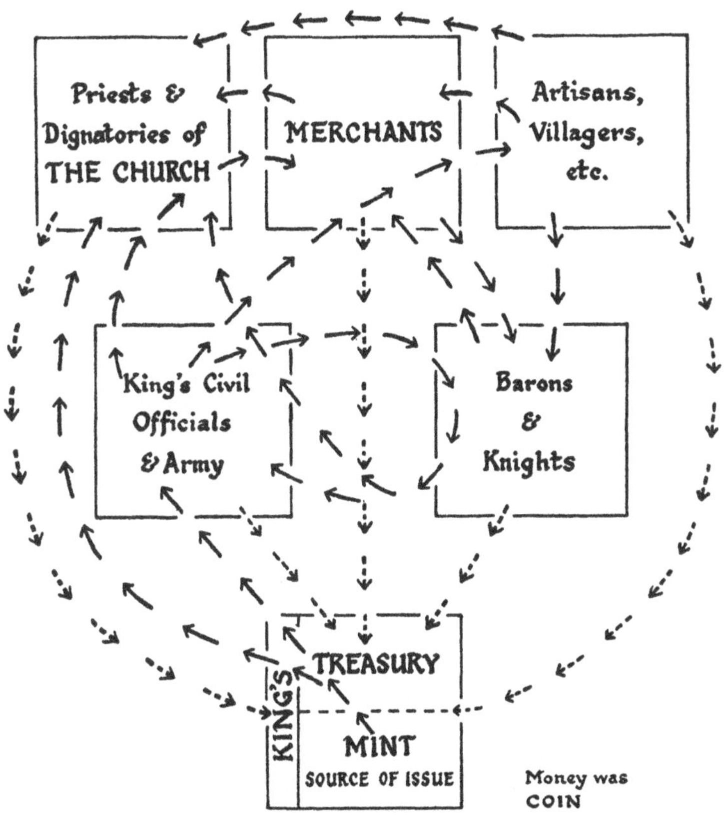

CIRCULATION OF MONEY, MIDDLE AGES

thread came back to be woven into cloth on their own looms by hired weavers. There are 15th century ballads about 'Jack of Newbury' who is said to have owned 200 looms and employed 600 men, women and children in his 'factory.' The children

> "*were in poore array,*
> *And every one sat picking wool,*
> *The finest from the coarse to cull;*
> *Their number was seven score and ten,*
> *The children of poore silly men,*
> *And these, their labours to requite,*
> *Had every one a penny at night.*"[1]

Such employers of labour as Jack of Newbury were the pioneers of a great development in industry—the change from *individual* production to what is called *capitalist* production.[2] Let us clearly understand the aims of the capitalist producer. He wanted to produce much cloth, and by its sale to gain for himself more money than he could have gained as an ordinary master-craftsman. His scheme began with the spending of money—he purchased his looms. Then he bought his raw material at the lowest possible price—farmers would sell a little more cheaply to a buyer who was ready to take all they had to sell at once—paid his work-people the lowest possible wage; and sold his cloth at as high a price as he could get for it. The difference between the amount of money he paid out—his *costs*—and that which he obtained from the sale of the cloth—his *prices*—constituted his *profit*—his means of living and saving for future expenses and purchases. We should note that the new scheme depended on his being able to get wage-earners; these were mostly workers too poor to buy wool for themselves. In that it increased the quantity of woollen cloth available for use in a country

[1]Thos. Deloney, *Works*. [2]See Note.

where the population was increasing, the new system was advantageous; but it brought with it disadvantages which you may perhaps guess, and which will presently become very clear.

The capitalists disliked the Gilds. The Gilds, with their fixed scales of payment for work, and their agreed 'just price' for the sale of cloth, got in the way of capitalist aims. So the capitalists left the towns and built loom sheds in the country. In the villages they found unemployed lads and girls (you remember how the conversion of arable to pasture land had reduced the number of field-labourers wanted) who thought how fine it was to learn a craft and earn a wage, even though the wage offered was very small. By thus carefully cutting down their costs of production the capitalists were able to sell large consignments of cloth to merchants at a lower price than that fixed by the Gilds, and yet make a good profit for themselves. And this was the beginning of a long struggle, between capitalists and Gilds, for the control of industry; for as soon as it was evident that cloth manufacturing capitalists were growing rich, the system was applied to other branches of manufacture. In the end the Gilds were broken up; but it is only fair to say that capitalism was not alone to blame. When towns grew large, and Craft Gilds numbered their members by thousands, Gild councils and the more influential Masters began to use the Gilds for their own advantage, and the earlier equality and justice between Gild members passed away.

Silk was spun and woven in London during the 14th and 15th centuries, this work mostly being done by women. It was a luxury fabric, only worn by the wealthy. Linen was a home-made product on some of the larger farms, where flax was grown; but Scotch and Irish linens were more frequently marketed. The spinning and weaving of cotton was introduced into Lancashire during the 16th century; but cotton did not come into common use for another hundred years. In 1720 an Act of Parliament forbade the wearing of calico, lest people should buy less woollen cloth, and in consequence English farmers and all concerned in the woollen industry should earn less money. For by this time there was no relation at all between the amount of cloth (or other commodity) made, and the quantity required for use by the people of the country as a whole. Manufacture for *use* had given place to manufacture for *sale*. England was becoming a 'nation of shop-keepers,' whose goods were prepared exclusively for people who possessed money. So a large part of the country's population, unable to buy, remained in need and want, while an increasing amount of produce was sold abroad.

Throughout the centuries we are surveying, the useful metals were smelted and manufactured, first by individual craftsmen and groups of craftsmen owning their small plant and tools, and then, later, by wage earners directed by capitalist owners. In the neighbourhood of Newcastle coal was dug with picks and spades from shallow surface pits, but the use of this fuel was limited to fires for warmth. Wood was used for smelting. The charcoal burners of the Middle Ages lived in little forest villages, where they calcined wood in rude kilns and sold it to the iron-smelter and the blacksmith. The furnaces of the iron-smelters were also located in forest areas and when, in the 16th century, the market demand for iron considerably increased, there was great wastage of the trees. The early smelter's method was to pack his rough stone furnace with a cone of ore, charcoal and wood in layers, apply bellows worked by hand or foot to a hole near the base, and maintain the draught until the ore was melted and could be run out into troughs of sand prepared for it. The bars or 'pigs' of iron so obtained were bought by the smith who, at his forge, with fire, hammer and water, and the superior power of his well-trained muscles, turned out implements of wrought iron or steel. When the iron-smelter found, during the 14th century, that he could make a water-wheel work more powerful bellows, his industry took a step forward; but when the much fiercer heat produced by coal fires had been tested, and combined with a cone of increased height, iron-smelting passed out of the hands of the individual craftsman, and presently became a complex process served by many workers.

CHAPTER VIII

A CHAPTER ON COINAGE AND TAXATION

WE have seen that the Greek state of Lydia, in Asia Minor, was the first community to make and use the device of coined money. The earliest coins were small oval lumps of electrum. They proved convenient both to buyer and seller, making unnecessary the tedious business of settling barter values—how many jars of oil, for instance, were worth a consignment of timber or marble—and also the equally tedious one of testing and weighing bars of metal. Each coin, being of declared weight, and bearing the stamp of the king or other authority issuing it, was guaranteed by the reputation of the issuer. The receiver of the coins could always demand that they should be weighed in his presence or tested for alloy if he suspected their quality; and no doubt this was usual as long as they were a novelty; but when they had become the common medium of exchange the majority of people accepted them at their face value. One drawback, indeed, the earlier coins had —they could easily be *clipped* by coinage thieves who with sharp files cut shavings from their edges, melted down the shavings and sold the metal. So carefully was this done that clipped coins frequently remained in circulation undetected for years, passing from hand to hand in exchange for goods, and serving precisely the same purpose as full-weight coins until some vigilant banker weighed them and refused to credit the customer bringing them for deposit with more than their weight value. When the *milled edge* was introduced into the process of coin minting, clipping became almost impossible.

It must be understood that the early coins passed freely only within the domain or area of the king or other authority issuing them. In Europe, during the Middle Ages, if Baron A. chose to issue a coin containing more lead than silver, and pay his dependents with such coins, they would circulate in his town and on his lands, serving the same purpose as if they were pure silver. But in Bishop B's town, perhaps thirty miles away, citizens would refuse to take Baron A's coins at face value in payment for goods. They would accept the coins only in bulk, according to the weight of the silver in composition. On the other hand, did Bishop B's money contain a larger proportion of silver, the citizens of Baron A's town would readily take it; but it would soon find its way into the Baron's melting pot.

Silver pennies were the coins generally used in Europe throughout the Middle Ages. The emperor KARL THE GREAT (Charlemagne) retained as a royal monopoly the issue of coinage, but this general control of money-making ceased after his death, and the feudal lords struck coins as they pleased. In England silver pennies were used from the days of the Saxon king OFFA; and English money of the Middle Ages was generally esteemed for its good silver weight. Two hundred and forty English silver pennies weighed a pound when new; the pennies were called 'esterlins,' and from their name we get the later word *sterling*, denoting reliability. For a pound weight of pennies an exchange coin was later struck in *gold*—the sovereign. It was a good thing for English trade abroad that English money contained so little alloy; it won the confidence of merchants by its purity. The exportation of silver, both coins and plate, was discouraged by English laws of the Middle Ages, in order that an adequate supply should circulate within the country.

During the 16th century the Spaniards and Portuguese brought large quantities of silver to Europe from mines in Peru and Mexico. Much of this silver was coined, and hence the amount of silver money circulating in European countries was considerably increased. This was not the case with the food and other commodities for sale. The result was that people soon found they had to pay more money for their goods—prices rose.[1]

It is important that we should understand why this happened, why it was bound to happen, and why it happens every time the quantity of money available suddenly increases while the quantity of goods for sale remains as before. The new silver quickly benefited a relatively few persons, its discoverers and the princes and other authorities who first placed it in circulation. It gave the latter the opportunity of paying their debts and of buying stocks of food and furnishings for their courts and armies. The demand thus made on the markets by such authorities reduced the quantity of goods available for other people, and merchants whose supplies were running short sold the remainder at higher prices. When two persons attempt to buy the same article the one bidding the higher price gets it, unless its price is fixed by law; prices therefore rose, generally. Nor was this rise limited to the prices of goods—landlords, finding the incomes they derived from the rent of their lands would buy less than formerly, raised rents. But wages rose little, or not at all; it is easy to see that the employer, obliged to pay more for his seed, stock, or raw materials, would not pay more also for labour unless compelled to do so. The increase in the supply of money due to the discovery of the American silver mines not merely did not benefit the wage earner—it left him worse off than before. The poorer classes were unable to buy as much food and clothing as formerly.

In this same century King Henry VIII debased the

[1]See Note.

English coinage. By his command the very small amount of alloy mixed with the silver was increased, until only four ounces in twelve of the metal coined were pure silver. This was convenient for the king, and since his coins were legal tender[1] made no immediate difference to trade within the country, but it was bad for merchants engaged in foreign trade. The merchant buying Dutch or French goods would probably have to pay for them in Dutch or French money; and at the exchangers' the king's head stamped on the coins counted for nothing—all that counted was the weight of real silver in the coins tendered for exchange. Foreign goods therefore cost three or four times as much in English money as before the coinage was debased.

Meanwhile, the English silver pennies of the Middle Ages had been succeeded by a variety of gold and silver coins. The golden *florin* and *noble* and the silver *groat* of EDWARD III (14th cent.) were followed by the *angel*, a fine gold coin, of EDWARD IV (15th cent.). HENRY VII, the first Tudor king, introduced the golden *sovereign* and silver *shilling*. Queen ELIZABETH issued better silver money and also copper coins, and made an attempt to recall the base coinage of her father, Henry VIII. Coins with milled edge were first struck in England in 1562, but another century passed before this method of checking the abuse of clipping was fully recognised. A copper coinage came into general use during the reign of JAMES I, and half-pence and farthings of copper from the end of the 17th century.

If we regard the king's government as the main source of the issue of money—and although this is *not* actually the case now it was so throughout the greater period of English history—we can look upon *taxation* as the means whereby a larger or smaller portion of the coins issued were returned to their source. The coins issued repre-

[1]See Note.

sented *purchasing power*—the power of purchasing goods and the services of other men. This purchasing power, issued from the king's mints, was never at any time distributed evenly among his subjects. It passed first into the hands of those who directly or indirectly supplied the king with what he needed for civil administration, for war, and for his personal life: thence it was handed on to other classes of the community in exchange for the products of their land or labour. But all subjects found themselves obliged to return to the king a portion of the money thus received, a contribution towards the *purchasing power* of the king's government. The wisest kings adjusted this *taxation* so as to impede as little as possible the work and trade of the nation, suiting the amount to the citizen. The imposition of a Poll Tax,[1] such as that levied in 1380 to pay war-time expenses, caused such hardship to the peasants that they were ready to kill the commissioners sent to collect it—the sum required per man being a small matter to the wealthy, but the equivalent of three or four days' wages to the cottar. This was the clumsiest form of taxation. Here is a list of other forms, more or less skilful.

(a) Feudal Dues—Scutage, Tallage and Aids.
(b) The Tenth and Fifteenth.
(c) Customs.
(d) Excise.
(e) Individual Property Taxes.

The feudal taxes were the demands of the king, as supreme landlord, upon his tenants-in-chief, the barons. We have seen that these latter originally held their land in return for war-service, and were bound by their agreement with the king to lead a company of armed men to fight as he desired for a certain number of days each year. Under this system the king's army was composed of many separate feudal units, having periods of service which began and ended

[1]One shilling per head.

at irregular times, the whole being on this account difficult to command. HENRY II decided that it would be more convenient to commute the war service of his tenants-in-chief for a money payment, with which he could hire mercenary soldiers when they were wanted; bands of men who made war their trade and would hire themselves out to fight for any leader of repute were numerous in Europe. Such money payment in lieu of military service was generally known as *scutage*; and thereafter scutage was levied at intervals by successive English kings till the year 1332.

Tallage was taxation; the king's tallage being generally taxation of the royal towns and of Jews. *Aids* were special levies according to feudal custom due to the king from the tenants-in-chief on the occasion of his daughter's marriage, the knighting of his elder son, etc. These forms of taxation had fallen largely into disuse by the end of the 14th century.

The tenth-part was a tax which had its origin in Jewish history; it was the contribution (in kind) of the Jewish household to the priest. The Church adopted it as the contribution (in corn and live-stock) asked of Christians—this was called *tithe*. In 1188 King HENRY II introduced a tax in this form. Every subject was required to pay value in coin of a tenth of his goods, stock, house and furniture; certain necessaries, such as the priest's books and the knight's armour being excepted. This tax was levied also by later kings.

Meanwhile Parliament, the king's council of barons, knights and burgesses was slowly establishing the right to affirm or deny the king's demand for new taxation. It became customary for the king to ask Parliament to grant revenues and for Parliament to impose taxes in the king's name. In 1334 an assessment was made of the value of all property in the kingdom, and from the total it was estimated that a tax of *one-tenth* on the townsmen, and of *one-fifteenth* on the county people, would realise a sum of £39,000 for the king. And, curiously, a century later, when Parliament voted 'a tax of one-tenth and one-fifteenth' it was actually granting the king £39,000 without any reference to the property values as they then stood. In each county the Sheriff was the king's officer responsible for the collection of the tax.

Customs, in the 12th century as now, are taxes levied on goods entering or leaving the kingdom. But while at the present time these taxes are mostly levied on *imports*, the merchants of the 12th and 13th centuries paid more for taking goods *out* of the country. Exported wool, cloth, hides, tin and lead were taxed in the reign of EDWARD I; and wine, imported from France, paid duty in kind, one cask in every ten being regarded as the king's property. Foreign merchants paid more both for export and import than English subjects. The rate of payment fixed by the parliament of EDWARD I remained substantially the same for nearly two centuries; but special levies of tonnage and poundage[1] were sometimes sanctioned. Merchants were required to pay the taxes to the king's officers of the Customs at the ports; by landing the goods secretly at lonely places on the coasts it was possible to evade payment, and smuggling was a craft respected and profitably pursued by coast-dwellers. Tonnage and poundage for life were voted at their accession to the Tudor monarchs and to JAMES I.

Excise was first levied in the 17th century. It is the tax paid by merchants on certain goods produced within the kingdom. Salt, malt, and distilled liquors were subjected to excise duty by the Long Parliament in CHARLES I's reign. The new tax was hated by the people, who feared it would be extended to other classes of goods; and salt was presently freed. After the death of CROMWELL a parliament composed of a majority of great land-owners came into power; they

[1]See Note.

recalled Charles Stuart, son of the late king, and crowned him, but took the opportunity to repeal the old feudal laws by which they were expected to pay dues for their land. To make up for the sum thus denied, they voted the king and his heirs Hereditary Excise on all ales, distilled liquors, and beers. The effect of both customs and excise duties is, of course, to raise the price to the consumers of the taxed goods, the merchants in this way passing on the tax to the public—so the landowners thus handed over the payments, formerly due from them, to the mass of the nation. . . . In 1733 the statesman ROBERT WALPOLE made an attempt to substitute a more general scheme of excise duties for those of the customs, which he proposed to abolish, on the grounds that they were easily evaded, and costly and difficult to collect. Owners of land had been paying, since 1692, a yearly *land tax* of 4s. per acre in war time and from 3s. to 1s. in time of peace—this tax Walpole hoped to reduce by making an increase in the revenues obtained by the increased excise. But by this time Britain had a large population of consumers who had no interest in land, and who objected strongly to seeing a rise in the prices of the goods chosen for excise—their opposition was effective in defeating Walpole's scheme.

Many taxes have from time to time been levied on *individual property*. As we have noted, the 'tenth' and 'fifteenth' partly took this form. So did the *subsidies* of Tudor reigns—which were raised by levies on land and on 'movable' goods other than clothing in use. People of the later 17th century paid a 'hearth' tax, imposed on the owners or tenants of all houses but cottages—it reduced the number of warmed rooms in dwellings; this was followed by a 'window' tax, which resulted in the blocking up or painting out of windows. In 1694 stamp duties were first imposed on legal documents such as receipts, contracts, bills of sale, etc.

In summary we observe:

1. That the KING, as war-leader and supreme land-owner of feudal times, formerly controlled both the issue of coin and its return to him by taxation.

2. That the king's function as war-leader became less necessary, and his absolute power lessened, while that of his council of tenants-in-chief and leading burgesses increased. That this council, Parliament, eventually succeeded in claiming and maintaining the right,

(a) to grant or veto taxes proposed by the king,

(b) to divert money from the king's treasury for purposes of government,

and finally,

(c) to make the king an allowance for his personal needs, and to control in its own interests both taxation and the spending of the money gathered by taxation.

It is frequently assumed that parliament represents the whole nation, and that therefore it collects and spends the revenue according to the national will. But this is only true in the sense that members of parliament are elected by groups of persons who expect these members to further the group interests. Land-owners vote for candidates who will oppose the taxation of land and ensure them the maximum freedom of action in dealing with their tenants in matters of rents, etc. Manufacturers and traders vote for candidates who will use their influence to extend trade and increase the making of profit by trade. Wage-earners vote for candidates who promise legislation in favour of higher wages and better conditions of labour. The result is what we call 'party' government—each party pushing its own claims, contesting or ignoring those of the other parties, and aiming to gain and hold for as long as possible a majority of the parliamentary seats, since by the right of this majority it controls the power of law-making and taxation formerly held by the king.

CHAPTER IX

SIX CENTURIES OF EUROPEAN TRADE

DURING the 12th and 13th centuries there were no better trodden roads in Europe than those leading to the small French province of *Champagne*. For within this province had grown up a series of fairs, so well-known that they drew merchants from all parts of Europe. The fairs were centred in the four little towns —*Troyes* the largest—of the Counts of Champagne; each fair lasted several weeks, and the series occupied nearly the whole year. We may therefore regard the Champagne fairs as the international market of these two centuries. To this market came the *surplus* goods of medieval producers—goods that could not be sold at a favourable price in the locality of their origin. Among the 'foreign' goods offered for sale were jewels, spices, a variety of textiles, wrought metals and leather, furs, Moorish weapons and negro slaves.

At the Champagne fairs merchant dealt with merchant as well as with private customer. The products of the East were exchanged for those of the West. As the popularity of the fairs grew, the Counts of Champagne became rich men—not because they traded themselves, but because they charged merchants high rates for tolls and booth sites, and required all payments to be made in their own money, the silver pennies of their own coining. Exchangers of money, having paid the Counts handsomely for the licence to set up a 'banc' or exchange counter, did not fail to extract their commission from the fair-going public.

Towns of the Middle Ages were of Roman or Saxon origin, such as Mainz or Canterbury; or kings' and barons' towns, which had begun as villages of artisans and craftsmen adjacent to the castle of the land-owner, such as Kingston and Warwick. A third class were those grown up around a large monastery or abbey, or the palace of a bishop. The first-named were often ruled by a high dignitary of the Church, the second by their king or baron, the third by abbot or bishop: in all cases they were regarded as a source of income by the overlord. Tolls were collected at the gates on goods entering and leaving; strangers entering also had to pay; a market or fair could be held only by special charter for which the townsmen paid. In this country the larger fairs were the prerogative of the king, and profits made formed part of his income.

All through the Middle Ages we find the townsmen striving to gain, little by little, the right to conduct independently the affairs of their town. Enterprising citizens achieved this by saving money earned by the practice of their crafts, and offering it to the overlord when he was in special need, in return for charters of freedom—freedom to exercise more or less control over the town's conduct and trade. Sometimes such charters were granted only for a time, sometimes bought outright, and recorded on parchments carefully kept in chests in the Gild Hall. Or the rights acquired by the council of burgesses might be partial and temporary, as in the case of Winchester where, during the fair of St. Giles, the bishop overlord of the city retained the keys, levied the tolls, set up his own court and, till the fair was ended, entirely superseded the municipal authorities.

Within the towns grew up the Gilds Merchant, each town having its own Gild. The Gild Merchant was a local trade union, which organised the trade of the town in the interests of the burgesses, who were in the beginning, it must be understood, the artisans and craftsmen themselves. Their regulations jealously excluded non-citizens from participation in ordinary trade. (The Gilds Merchant preceded the Craft Gilds, the latter developing later, when the towns had grown larger.)

Transport of goods was a slow, difficult and expensive matter throughout the Middle Ages. The means of conveyance were the pack-horse or mule, the rough cart, and the small sailing boat or barge. Every bridge and ford belonged to a land-holder who exacted toll. The majority of roads were little better than tracks, rutted in the summer, boggy in the winter. Robbers abounded, and the barons themselves were not slow to seize merchants' wares upon slight pretext. Under such conditions the travelling merchant or pedlar led a life which was both adventure and gamble. Yet international trade nevertheless slowly increased.

Merchants formed Defence Gilds. The Gilds hired soldiers to guard their merchandise on its way from fair to fair, and armed ships to convoy it from port to port. Thus came into being the medieval trading leagues known as the Hanses. The *Flemish* Hanse was an association of Flemish and English merchants who for two centuries controlled all the trade between London and the towns of Flanders. Armour, glass and woven fabrics floated across to England on the frail, high-decked ships of the time; and English wool went to Flanders. "In the 14th century England was practically the only source of wool for western Europe."[1] (We have seen how King Edward III discouraged this export of wool, with a view to increasing the manufacture of cloth in England; in his reign it was possible for merchants to send English-woven *cloth* abroad paying a duty of only 2%, while the duty on wool amounted to nearly a third of its value).

Larger and more powerful than the Flemish Hanse

[1] C. M. Waters, *Economic History of England.*

was the Northern Hanse or *Hanseatic League*. It was a union of the merchants of Cologne, Hamburg, Bremen, Wisby, Lubeck, the Russian free city of Novgorod, and the ports of Norway and Sweden. This league of traders controlled and monopolised the buying and selling of all the products of the north, fish, fur, timber and hides. It permitted no non-member to send merchant or fishing vessels into the Baltic Sea; it kept a fleet of war-ships, and was strong enough to defy the Danish kings who attempted to limit its monopoly. It became very rich in coin, and we read of it making war-loans to fighting princes—Edward III of England among them. The League's ships sailed up the Thames and landed their cargoes at the wharf of the *Steelyard*, a walled enclosure containing offices, warehouses and the dwelling of the Governor who, by permission of the English kings, lived there in armed state.

The Crusades of the 11th and 12th centuries, with their call to the Holy Land, brought barons and knights with their companies from northern and western Europe to Constantinople, Venice, Marseilles and Genoa. The merchants of these and other ports provided the Crusading armies with food and transport; and since the demand was urgent, the prices charged were high. Jew and Lombard bankers made loans at interest to Crusaders, the latter often pledging lands or jewels as security; if the borrowers returned no more, the bankers waited on their heirs for the security so pledged, and a great deal of wealth passed into money-lenders' hands in this way.

One result of the Crusades was the spread into western Europe of a desire for Oriental products. The northern barons and their following, while living in touch with Greek, Italian and Syrian peoples, acquired a taste for silk and velvet clothing, worked leather shoes, jewelled ornaments and weapons, drugs and spices—a great variety of things previously unknown to them.

Such goods they brought back to England, Flanders and Germany, thus creating a market for them in the northern lands. But again we note that the foreign merchant ready to sell such goods was not disposed, as a rule, to barter them. He preferred to be paid in coin, which was convenient to carry—or better still, since robbers were many, he liked a document authorising a well-known merchant of his own country to make payment to him in coin on his return home. Italian and Jewish merchants began to act as bankers for wealthy northerners who wanted to buy goods from the Mediterranean countries and Asia. They appointed trusted agents in northern towns to receive monies on deposit from their customers, and to exchange these monies for the currency of other towns or countries as desired. They also would make loans at interest to persons who possessed houses, land or jewels to pledge as security; or to a king or other authority in return for some privilege or monopoly.

The merchant fleets of the Venetians that proved so useful during the Crusades as transport for the armies, later became famous for their long trading voyages. In the 13th and 14th centuries Venetian galleys would sail, as many as five hundred together, for the Black Sea, Egypt, Syria, or westward between the Pillars of Hercules, and across the Bay of Biscay. The Flanders galleys passed up the English Channel and anchored off Bruges. Venetians also traded with the far East. MARCO POLO, son of a 13th century Venetian merchant, has told the story of adventures with his father and uncle on a memorable journey to the court of the great Chinese emperor KUBLA KHAN.[1] But there was no *general* trade carried on over such long routes during the Middle Ages; only luxury goods—jewels, rare curios, silks, the merchandise of kings and the very wealthy—found their way to Europe from the far East.

[1] *The Travels of Marco Polo.*

The first of oriental products to come into general use in western Europe was *spice*. We noticed in a previous chapter that since only a small inadequate supply of fodder for winter use was grown, nearly all meat eaten in winter was of the salted or preserved variety. Hence there was a big demand for spices—pepper, cloves, ginger, cinnamon, etc., which disguised the flavour of the frequently tainted winter joint or pasty. Early in the 16th century Portuguese sailors began to bring spices from India and the East Indies by sea direct to Lisbon, the Portuguese explorer VASCO DA GAMA having discovered a route to India via the African Cape of Good Hope. This spice trade was very profitable to the Portuguese, whose method of obtaining what they wanted from the natives was little better than robbery. Later they lost the trade to the Dutch, who established fortified trading depots in the East Indies.

Silk and *paper* were manufactured exclusively in China until the 13th century. Later, both were produced in Italy and France, and were exported thence to the other western countries. The increase in the supply of writing material helped the spread of written knowledge; previously this had been greatly hampered by the scarcity and expense of parchment.

The *standard of life* in England continued slowly to rise. What do we mean by that? The standard of life is said to be *low* in a community if its people generally have little material wealth, enjoying neither variety nor abundance of goods. It is *high* when a considerable majority of the people enjoy both variety and abundance. During the Middle Ages there was sometimes scarcity and sometimes a temporary abundance, but never great variety of foods, while for all but the small minority of nobles and wealthy merchants clothing was scarce and dear. Throughout the 15th, 16th, and 17th centuries we note an increase in the material wealth of the country, shared by a larger number of its population. Instead of a minority of land-owners, able to command the best their land produces, and a majority of peasants sharing the rest of the produce more or less equally, there are three classes of people—those whose wealth exceeds what they can consume, a middle class of traders enjoying both variety and abundance, and those in poverty. From the two upper classes comes a continually rising demand for goods from abroad.

This demand is met by the trading companies that in the 16th and 17th centuries take the place of the Hanses of the Middle Ages. We read of the Dutch and English East India Companies, the Merchant Adventurers, the Muscovy and Turkey Companies. Between these and the earlier trading associations are differences which indicate the widening outlook of merchants' minds. The Hanseatic League was a union of independent or semi-independent *cities*, Flemish, German, Russian, Scandinavian and English—each city being a trading unit. But bigger trading units—the modern nations—were coming into existence during the 16th century. The Russian and Scandinavian cities were conquered by powerful princes, and lost their independent status; religious persecution and the Thirty Years' War weakened the others in Europe. In England a national sentiment grew and deepened. It began to matter less to a man what town he lived in. The merchant's *country* was what mattered abroad; and the Bristol trader was ready to enter into agreement with the London trader because they were both Englishmen.

The trading associations of the 16th and 17th centuries were, therefore, national in character. The *Dutch East India Co.* was indeed an association of cities—but of Dutch cities. Each Dutch state contributed towards the company's capital and shared in the trade and profits. Batavia, in the East Indies, was the Asiatic headquarters, where a strong armed force was kept. The company's ships carried cannon as well as cargo, and frequently came into conflict with Portuguese traders, whom it eventually drove away from Ceylon and Malacca. The *English East India Co.* was established later, receiving a charter from Queen Elizabeth in 1600; the charter gave officials of this company the sole right (as far as English merchants were concerned) of trading with all countries lying beyond the Cape of Good Hope or the Straits of Magellan. The *Muscovy Co.* held a similar monopoly of trade between England and Russia, Armenia, and the lands around the Caspian Sea. The *Turkey Co.* sent its ships to the eastern Mediterranean with cargoes of cloth, and brought back drugs and raw silk. The *Merchant Adventurers* claimed the trade on the Rhine and the Elbe.

All these companies aimed at keeping a certain area of foreign trade in the hands of their own members. Merchants trading independently ran the risk of infringing a company's monopoly, and of being fined or imprisoned. If the merchant joined a Regulated Company, such as the Merchant Adventurers, he shipped his own cargo and was responsible for its profits or losses, but had certain advantages of marketing, and the assistance of the Company's agents in foreign countries. The *Joint Stock* Companies, such as the English East India Company, worked differently. Each member contributed a share of money to the common capital, and received a share of the profits made by a voyage; but the whole of the business of transporting and exchanging goods, buying and selling, was carried out by the company's paid employees. A council or board of the chief shareholders appointed the more responsible employees, the organisers of the trade. The East India Company, at its foundation, was composed of 125 members, merchants who collectively subscribed for it a capital of £72,000. It established 'factories' which were really receiving houses for native goods, at Surat, Madras, Bombay, and at the mouth of the Ganges; and its agents sought to acquire privileges and rights over territory from the native princes. From the beginning it came into conflict with the Dutch East India Comapny; fighting took place when ships of the rival companies met.

The voyages of COLUMBUS to the West Indies turned the minds of adventurers and traders towards the prospect of wealth to be acquired beyond the Atlantic Ocean. Columbus's expedition had been blessed by the Spanish monarchs Ferdinand and Isabella; and subsequently Spanish galleons were ready to sail to the newly discovered lands in search of treasure. Here there was no development of real trade, which is a reasonable exchange of goods, but merely compulsion of the natives to collect and ship silver. Nor was there any general distribution of the metal when it reached Spain; ship-masters and officials secured shares, some went to the royal mint—but much more to Flemish, Italian and German bankers in payment of interest on loans they had made previously to Spanish monarchs.[1] Real trade between Europe and America began only after the various groups of European pioneers, who emigrated to America in the 16th and 17th centuries, had explored and cultivated lands on the eastern seaboard of that continent.

[1]In 1560 these loans amounted to about £20,000,000, with accumulation of interest at from 15% to 30%.

CHAPTER X

THE ARTIST IN THE ECONOMIC WORLD

THIS book concerns itself with man's past and present struggle for economic freedom—his general movement through the ages towards a condition in which the primary needs, food, clothing and shelter, shall be ensured to the race by other means than the enforced labour of its majority. Science and invention have now made possible such a condition of freedom and leisure; and far-sighted thinkers of all nations welcome the true and real abolition of slavery; yet because the possibility is still new and strange to the slower-moving mind of the general public, there are not lacking persons who regard it with dislike—even with fear. Fear lest the body of the world's workers, the millions now compelled to a monotony of daily labour uncongenial and personally unprofitable (except as means to wage-earning) should become lazy, useless, vicious, if this compulsion were withdrawn.

Such apprehension might be justifiable if man's nature was such that he could be content with the right to eat, drink and warm himself. But these are only his primary needs; he has others, waiting till the first are supplied. Healthy children, reared in a well-provided home, accept their meals, clothes, the house and garden as a matter of course, and turn their energy to account in doing a multitude of things which are *practice in living*, and part of the process of their education. So will it be with mankind in a state of economic freedom. Children, being young, immature things, may not know what it is they want to do, and until they find out for themselves they may be temporarily fretful. They may experiment in wasteful and annoying fashion with materials provided for their use. But they will ultimately, unless frustrated by the stupidity of an interfering authority, find channels for their accumulating energy, and turn it to new and valuable achievement. Man does not leave work behind him with the Age of Scarcity; he abandons a state of slavery under the whip of economic necessity for one of free co-operation and individual choice.

The mind of man is creative and inventive. Hitherto the creative and inventive faculties of the million have been mainly employed in securing a 'living,' either directly, as by hunting or agriculture, or by gaining money to exchange for the primary necessities. There has been little time or energy to spare for Art, which is the expression of the creative impulse, or for Invention, unless the latter assisted the getting of wealth.

Art persisted from earliest times under check and sufferance. Painted pottery succeeded the rough clay vessels, and the carved portico the portal of hewn timber. Drawing pointed the way to writing, and the mud tablet records of ancient Sumer to the parchments of Alexandria and the leathern tomes of the medieval monasteries. Did the Chaldean observer, patiently mapping the changing aspects of day and night from his temple tower, work less surely in the interests of man than the ploughman cutting his furrows in the plain below? A long, slow development of human thought unites the architects of the Egyptian pyramids with Euclid and Archimedes, and Ptolemy with Copernicus, Galileo and Newton; it was only possible because the mathematicians were freed from the obligation to do manual labour. Poets and philosophers, devoted to the search for beauty and truth, win for the spirit of man as real an advance in freedom, scope of knowledge and opportunity, as is secured for him in physical fact by the explorers who have given the whole world into his possession.

But science and art must build upon a basis of economics. By which we mean that the imaginative and inventive powers can only be fully exercised when the mind is relieved of the necessity for concentrating upon provision of food, clothing and shelter. In early ages science and art were of necessity *incidental*, subsidiary to the main business of material production. Within the primitive community only the priests and bards, supported by the labour and gifts of the people, were able to devote their time and energy to thought, the acquisition of new knowledge, and the perception of beauty. As long as a tribe or nation is compelled to spend all but a moiety of its strength in producing the materials on which its physical life depends, or in defending its possessions, it cannot develop the higher mental powers or attain to a fine culture. If its wealth and security increase it is able to spare an increasing amount of energy for mental pursuits, invention, scientific investigation, and the arts. Generations of settlement in the fertile Euphrates and Nile deltas gave to Sumerians and Egyptians respectively the opportunity of developing a high standard of artistic work, of nature knowledge expressed in myth, and of astronomical science. No such culture was possible among the striving nomad tribes.

Yet the nomads esteemed and supported that primitive artist the bard.

> "When there appeared a poet in a family of the Arabs, the other tribes round about would gather to that family and wish them joy of their good luck. Feasts would be got ready, the women of the tribe would join together in bands, playing upon lutes, as they were wont to do at bridals, and the men and boys

would congratulate one another; for a poet was a defence to the honour of them all, a weapon to ward off insult from their good name, and a means of perpetuating their glorious deeds."[1]

The poet-priest of the Aryan Indians received tribal tribute like the king. The support of the priesthood was a first charge on all early civilised communities, because the priests were regarded as the indispensable intermediaries between gods and men. The leisure thus gained by the priestly class was frequently occupied in the pursuit of knowledge and the arts. This was notably the case in Egypt and Babylonia.

"*The cost of production is consumption.*" We can profitably consider here this economic axiom. The actual cost of any object or enterprise is just the amount of material wealth consumed in the process of its production or accomplishment. The cost of a cabinet made by a craftsman is actually nothing more or less than the food, clothing and shelter the craftsman uses while the work is in progress, together with the wear of his tools and the materials utilised for the job. The cost of a war, over and above the waste of human and animal life, is the total amount of the goods and commodities consumed by the armies engaged, whether usefully, as food, clothing, shelter and transport, or destructively, as by the action of high explosive. And the cost of a work of art is all that contributes to the life of the artist.

Throughout the Age of Scarcity (which includes all periods of history before the application of steam and electric power to machinery) human communities were of necessity obliged to regard the creative work of the artist as luxury production, less indispensable than agriculture and the crafts. Time and energy spent upon artistic pursuits represented a loss upon the amount available for the production and defence of material

[1]Ibn Rashig, trans. Sir Charles Lyall.

goods. The primitive tribe might support a priest-poet or bard, but only the settled, civilised people with its store of accumulated wealth could support a whole priesthood at leisure.

The artist of the early civilisations, unattached to the priesthood, had no place except as a dependent of the 'big house' man. He lived in the household or court of his patron, not infrequently as a slave, and in any case subject to the caprice of those from whom he received sustenance. At a later stage in the progress of a community such as that of the Athenian Greeks, who developed a rare culture and general love of artistic work, it became possible for the artist to support himself by exchanging his productions—his writings, songs, poems, the music of his lute or lyre, his pictures, sculpture or pottery, for the money which would buy him food and other necessaries. By selling his creations he could retain his individual freedom, and even (but rarely) acquire wealth. But whether the artist-merchant starved or gained affluence depended, and still depends, less upon the real value of his work than upon the current public demand for it; and since the greatest art is seldom understood or fully appreciated when it is first given to the world, the finest artists of the Age of Scarcity were poor men.

CHAPTER XI

MONEY AND BANKING BEFORE A.D. 1700

WE noticed how buyers and sellers, come to the Champagne fairs from all parts of Europe, were obliged to repair first to the money-changers' booths, where they exchanged coin of their own locality for the silver pennies of the Counts of Champagne. The money-changers weighed and tested the coin, and returned its equivalent value less a commission for their services. If people grumbled that the commission was a high one the money-changer would point to the licence he had bought from the Count's steward for the privilege of setting up his booth.

The money-changer was often also a usurer, and generally a Jew or a Florentine. The Jews, who were to be found in all cities, despised and avoided by the Christians, were not permitted to join the Craft Gilds, and therefore could not earn a living by any trade. Many of them turned to money-changing and lending. But dealers in money were not unknown among Christian peoples: the Lombard merchants of north Italy especially won riches and the contempt of Christendom by following the Jews' lead.

Hoarded money was a source of anxiety to the owner in days when thieves were bold and civic protection did not exist. The townsman carried his treasure to the wealthy goldsmith whose iron-clamped chests and guarded vault inspired confidence no less than his respected character. The merchant charged a fee for storing the money, and handed a receipt to its owner. Now we must note two developments.

The Church of the Middle Ages, as we have seen, discountenanced and forbade usury. The practice of lending money at interest was regarded throughout Christendom as a sin, and usurers as wicked persons or heathen. But slowly, after the 15th century, the Church lost its hold over men's minds, and practices it had condemned slipped back into accepted use.[1] The goldsmith of the 16th and 17th century, entrusted with the money of his fellow-citizens, found there was small risk and much gain to himself in lending the bulk of it to other customers for stated periods. Relatively few of his clients came on any single day to ask for their money back. Henceforward the would-be borrower might apply for a loan from the respected merchant in the High Street, the town councillor or alderman, instead of to the despised Jew in the Ghetto—and he liked it much better. The borrower had, of course, to furnish security and pay interest in either case, and the trouble was the same if, when his loan was called in, he could not return the money. But the transaction now seemed quite a respectable one. Only when a sudden emergency, such as the outbreak of war or the threat of invasion, caused a panic, and citizens rushed in a body to claim and take away their gold and silver, did people realise that the goldsmith's vaults were less safe than they appeared to be, and that the obliging banker had been loaning not his own coin but that of his customers.

The second development was that of the use, as money, of the goldsmith's receipts for coin deposited with him. Citizen M., who had deposited £100 and received a receipt for that amount, might later buy a consignment of wool worth £100 from merchant P. Instead of paying for this in coin, he might offer merchant P. his receipt. Merchant P. being confident of the

[1]Henry VIII first legalised usury in England.

goldsmith's integrity, and also of Citizen M's, might accept the receipt, believing that he had only to present it at the goldsmith's counter to receive Citizen M's gold. Or he might pass on the receipt to a third person in payment for goods. Exactly in this way goldsmiths' receipts for deposited coin, plate and bullion began to pass from hand to hand, bits of paper or parchment thus serving the same purpose as coin.

The early European banking houses were extensions of the money-changing business. As international trade increased, it was convenient for wholesale dealers to deposit sums of money intended for the payment of goods, at the house of a recognised banker living in a city upon the main trade route. The sums deposited were naturally in a large number of different currencies. To get over the difficulty of assessing exact values in terms of coins containing varying amounts of gold or silver, bankers issued 'bank money.' Each customer knew how much bank money his deposit was worth. Freights and consignments of goods could then be valued in terms of 'bank money,' and transfers made by the clerks from the deposits of the buyers to those of the sellers. Such a Bank of Exchange was founded in Amsterdam in 1609. There the traveller—from Denmark let us say—could 'buy' with his home currency money of the country whither he was bound.

A further service rendered by the bank was the 'discounting' of Bills of Exchange. These documents were (and are) used by merchants and producers buying and selling goods over a distance. Merchant X., in Copenhagen, wants a consignment of tobacco from Planter Y., in Havana. Both have deposits of money at the Exchange Bank. Planter Y., when dispatching his tobacco to Merchant X., sends also a bill of exchange; it runs something like this:

To the Bank of Exchange. *June 30th,* 1654.

£100

At six months date pay to our order the sum of One Hundred Pounds. Value received.
Signed:

This bill Merchant X. will sign as 'accepted' and return. When the time stated has elapsed, Planter Y., on presentation of the bill at the Havana branch of the Bank, can have one hundred pounds worth of Merchant X's money paid to him over the counter, or the same amount transferred from the latter's deposit to his own. But here again there was a further development. Planter Y. might be wanting money urgently before the six months were up. In that case he could take the bill to the banker, who would say: "This bill is not due for payment, but I will discount it for you"—and he would give Planter Y. £98, or perhaps a little more or less, but not the whole £100. Then when the date for payment arrived, £100 of Merchant X's money would be transferred to the banker's account, the latter gaining £2 or so by the transaction. This business of 'discounting' bills of exchange became very profitable, and we find firms known as 'discount houses' coming into being, their chief business the buying and selling by hundreds and thousands of these bills of exchange.

Money lenders were often called to the private audience rooms of kings whose expenditure exceeded the sums gathered from their subjects by taxation. CHARLES II of England began to borrow from London merchants at 8%, but so frequently did he apply for loans that they ultimately raised the rate of interest as high as 30%. Some of these loans were never repaid, and they formed the beginning of the English National Debt. We have observed that the Bank of

Amsterdam was an extension of the money-changers' business. We have now to show how the Bank of England, founded in 1694, was an extension of the London money-lenders' business.

King WILLIAM III was engaged in a European war which, in spite of the heavy taxation of the time, drained his treasury. To withdraw from the war would have been to admit defeat—William would not. His ministers sought to borrow money, and a clever Scotchman named WILLIAM PATERSON produced a scheme for the foundation of a new bank, which was presently adopted. Certain wealthy merchants of the city of London agreed to combine to lend a sum of £1,200,000 at 8% interest (not to the king in person but to the responsible ministers who formed, together with Parliament, the king's government). In return, they received a charter naming their company "the Corporation of the Bank of England," which Corporation was granted the sole right thereafter of making loans for government use. The annual interest on this first loan —about £100,000—was to form the capital of the company, which proposed both to invite deposits of coin and bullion from traders and private persons, and to lend to customers, not coin, but printed ***bank-notes*** which were promises to pay gold on demand. Permission was granted by the charter for the printing and issue of notes to the face value of £100,000. Here was a new departure! The founders of this Bank of England were in effect saying: "Since the country is short of coinage, and since also the merchants have become accustomed to using goldsmiths' receipts and bills of exchange as money, why should we not issue ***promises to pay***, and let them circulate as money too!" A pamphlet printed in 1697 stated: "The main purpose of banking is to furnish the kingdom with an imaginary coin to serve the purpose of that which is really so." The 'imaginary coin'—the bank-note—was accepted by the public, and passed from hand to hand in payment for goods and services. Each holder felt confident that he could at any time change his notes for gold over the counter of the Bank which received a large sum from the country's taxes every year. Paper money had come to stay. And the practice of usury, formerly discredited, was to be housed with honour in the highest places of the British nation.

In 1696 King William's ministers made another attempt to raise money for the expenses of the war. They issued Exchequer Bills. These were really a general invitation to British subjects to lend money at interest to the government. (The Bank of England Co.'s monopoly was in respect of business firms only.) Each Bill was a certificate stating that the holder had lent £10, and was entitled to interest at the rate of 3d. per day. The Bank of England company bought the bills and asked for an extension of its charter. Notice that we say 'bought' the bills! Regarding the yearly interest on them as certain to be paid, the company was prepared to 'market' the bills—that is, to sell them to customers who would pay £11 or more for the chance of receiving as much as 3d. a day on each bill. If you work out the percentage, you will find that at this high rate the buyer would receive more money back in interest within four years than he had originally paid. The king got the money for the war; the banking company made a substantial profit; the citizen with money to lend profited also; but it was all at the expense of the nation, which had to pay more for necessary articles of food and clothing, because these were taxed to increase the revenue.

From this time onward a recognised and approved trade in Bills of Exchange, Exchequer Bills, and debt certificates generally went on increasing. The headquarters in Britain of the trade was (and is) the London Money Market. The dealers in 'stocks and shares,' the 'jobbers' and 'brokers,' formed the Stock Exchange Company, trading under certain agreed conditions. To a citizen of the Middle Ages, such trade would have seemed fantastic, but later generations have become so accustomed to receive interest for money lent that we in our time accept it as a matter of course. We all borrow and lend, from the cabinet minister who negotiates a loan for millions of pounds' value on behalf of his government, to the child who lends pence to the Penny Banker for the sake of the penny or halfpenny of interest promised him annually on a shilling.

The Bank of England Company's charter, as revised in 1697 contained, among others, the following provisions.

1. The Company to have the monopoly of making loans to the Government for a further period of 13 years.

2. All sums due to the Government on account of revenue to be paid through the Bank.

3. The Company would make a second loan of over a million pounds value, at 8% interest, to the Government, which guaranteed to pay the interest out of the revenue obtained by the tax on salt.

4. No other joint stock bank should be permitted to come into being during the continuance of the Bank of England Company's monopoly.

CHAPTER XII

PRODUCTION, DISTRIBUTION, AND WAR

TO the nomad tribe of the dawn of history, concerned solely with the increase and defence of its possessions, war offered the direct alternative of gain or loss. In war the tribe measured its physical strength and the quality of its leadership against those of its opponent; and the victor in a battle added to its own possessions the property of the vanquished. Gain or loss was shared by all the free members of the tribe—not equally, but in proportion to their tribal status.

This was simple. But when tribes settled, and accumulated stores of goods, the matter became more complicated. Defence of the wealth possessed was now the first consideration; only when the citizens were reasonably satisfied that their city, fortified and guarded, could repulse raiders, would they willingly and whole-heartedly leave it to attack foreigners upon their own ground. Nor, if the Pharaoh, Lord of Egypt, made war, was the fighting a combined attack by all the men of the nation—it was the affair of the army, the professional military class. To this class belonged the credit of victory or the disgrace of defeat; and to this class accrued the spoils of war, other than those apportioned to the priesthood (in the name of the gods), and to the king-leader.

Preparations for a campaign against another city or nation increased the labours of the craftsmen, both freemen and slaves. The provisioning of the army reduced the surplus stores of food. When king and warriors, in all the exciting show of their war panoply had departed, the farmer returned to his fields and the artificer to his workshop, and their lives proceeded as usual until the fate of the campaign was decided, and the army either returned in triumph with captives and spoil, or straggled back as a defeated remnant. Definite victory meant fêtes and celebrations, general approval and rejoicing; but it also meant a full slave market. An influx of slaves was bad for the poor freemen who lived by the sale of their labour; employers would not hire freemen when very cheap slaves were to be bought—and the outcome of this was that the freemen and their families also sank to slavery, being compelled by extreme poverty to sell themselves. Repeatedly does history show us the sequel: a community with a small slave-owning class accumulating more wealth than it can consume or use, and a large irresponsible class not only enslaved but become slave-minded, having no ideal beyond winning the favour of its masters.

As long as the greater part of the world's population remained at its tribal stage of nomadic or barbarian village life, degenerate, slave-supported centres of civilisation were bound to fall, ultimately, to the attack of the nomads. Man lives and thrives by action, by the exercise of his powers. The wealthy citizen of the slave-run state tended less and less to action and more and more to luxury and enervation of body and mind; slaves could obey, but they were not good defenders—the slave mind cringes, it does not oppose. So Cyrus the Persian chief, seized Babylon, in its day the London of the world. So the city and empire of Rome lost their unity and prestige, and western Europe passed into the hands of semi-barbaric peoples whose period we designate by the name Dark Ages. For what is called the 'decline' of a civilisation is the degeneracy consequent upon its citizens' loss, in the greater part, of their economic freedom.

Out of the confusion of the Dark Ages arose the feudal

communities. By feudal custom the liege lord could only claim from his vassals a limited number of days' war service each year. The reason for this is clear—the fighters were also the producers. For the greater part of the year the weapons might hang in the hall; their owners were out upon the land, ploughing, sowing, harvesting; the blacksmith at his forge, the miller at his mill. It could not be otherwise in small, self-supporting communities such as the early feudal holdings. Man cannot fight unless he eat. King ALFRED THE GREAT, when he organised the men of his country of Wessex to withstand the attacks of the Danes, divided his *fyrd* or militia into two equal sections. Alternatively these served as coast defenders, and as producers of the nation's food supply.

The Crusades of the 11th and 12th centuries presented another situation. The strongest power in Europe was then the religious organisation of the Christian Church, headed by the bishops and cardinals; its power lay not in civil or military authority but in its influence over the minds of the people. When the Muhammadan Turks of western Asia moved towards Constantinople their action threatened this Christian dominance, and war against the Turks was preached from all the pulpits of Christendom. The great response to this war summons was due partly to increasing population; the field labour of nearly every member of the feudal communities was no longer necessary; and a class of professional soldiers was forming—unproductive persons, prepared only to make war, seize, and consume wealth. Peaceful work went forward more easily when these fighters, led by the crusading barons, went away to attack the Turks. The home populations were not called upon to feed them; transport was too primitive and difficult for armies to carry food over long distances. Crusading companies looted provisions, or purchased them when looting was impracticable. We have noted (Chap. IX) how the need of the Crusaders brought to the merchants and money-lenders of the Mediterranean ports a trade that enriched their cities. Also, since experience of eastern products gave Europeans a taste for such things, how another secondary result of the Crusades was a demand by the nobility of France, Flanders and England for Italian and Venetian fabrics, and for the spices of the East.

War kept the armourer busy, making new weapons, but also mending old ones. Before the age of firearms a man's weapons were his 'tools of defence.' Knife, sword, pike, lance, dagger—short of mischance these might last their owner's lifetime. A change came when in the 14th century gunpowder began to play a part in warfare. The cannon ball, the hand grenade, and all the explosive munitions that followed them were in no sense tools, nor had they individual owners. They were products manufactured to be consumed, and in their consumption to cause loss of life or property. In course of time the trade of the armourer was superseded by those of the gunsmith and the manufacturer of explosives. A state of war increased the demand for their goods, and therefore expanded their profits; they formed a class of persons who throve by destruction. Their trade was, and is, infinitely more to-day, a menace to every nation—a menace which will continue and increase until the peoples of the western world, speaking through their governments, or by the voice of a world council representing those governments, utterly forbid such trade.

There is a record of the use of gunpowder at the battle of Crecy, fought between English and French in 1346, when "with fire and a noise like God's thunder" wooden cannon "threw little iron balls to frighten the horses." From that time during the next four centuries the nature of war gradually changed. The hand-to-hand struggle of men at close quarters gave way to longer and longer range shooting. The general destruction of life and property proportionately increased with every succeeding campaign. It remained for the 19th and 20th centuries to apply electric power to machine weapons, and to turn warfare to massacre by the invention and use of high-explosive shells, bombs and torpedoes.

PART TWO

THE ERA OF SOLAR ENERGY AND MACHINE LABOUR

CHAPTER I

FIFTY SIGNIFICANT YEARS (A.D. 1750-1800)

THE second half of the 18th century saw the dawn of the Age of Plenty—the beginning of the era of mechanical power.

It was no benign, peaceful dawn, radiant with the promise of a fair day. Indeed, for multitudes living at the time, it seemed rather the descent into a night of poverty and distress darker than they had known before. Within the period of these fifty years we mark the Seven Years' War, which was not confined to Europe, but extended to the American colonies, Canada and India; the American War of Independence; the French Revolution and the European war that followed it. Each of these wars wasted man's wealth faster than he could by industry replace it.

Heroic characters and stirring events abounded. But in the long view of history the figure of JAMES WATT, quietly experimenting with his model engines, is more significant than that of all the statesmen and generals. In 1782, James Watt, whose mind had taken up the problem of the practical steam engine where THOMAS NEWCOMEN had left it, succeeded in making one which would indubitably drive the pistons of a pump. *A natural force, Steam, more powerful than human or animal muscular energy, had been harnessed to man's more complex tool—his machine.* It had been brought under complete control, which was not the case with wind and water, the natural forces previously utilised.

A small, clumsy steam pump, bringing water out of a

mine. Pumping up water without the aid of muscular power. That, in the year 1782, was the beginning of the unperceived Age of Plenty. In 1784, behold a steam engine sucking air into a blast furnace. A year or two later another one keeping in motion wheels and belts controlling the working of a spinning-jenny. More and more steam engines, applied to one after another of the processes of wool, cotton, iron manufacture. The mind of man thoroughly intrigued with his new discovery; dwelling upon it, concentrating upon further invention and improvement; absorbed in it to the exclusion of other equally important considerations. As result, a rapid increase in the quantity of manufactured goods and commodities for disposal. This, henceforth, is the general trend of economic history.

Let us look in more detail at the second half of the 18th century, and for a moment leave the strange new development of the steam-driven machine to visit the English countryside. In 1750 rural England still had its commons and its communal unenclosed shrub wastes, where cottars and small-holders grazed cows and fed geese. Arable cultivation was still mainly done on the strip system, with division of labour among the villagers at ploughing and harvest. This did not make for economy—the better workers were hampered by the worse ones, and the well-cleaned strip suffered from its proximity to that which was weedy and undrained. It was clear that the larger farms, under individual ownership, yielded better and heavier crops. Land-holders began to advocate dividing up the common land, so that it should all come under individual ownership; they argued, that if each and every farmer and cottar were put in absolute possession of his holding, the standard of cultivation would improve generally.

Legislation made it easy for the land-holders to obtain from Parliament permission to 'enclose' the land in any given area. All that was necessary was the consent of those who held the greater part of it already. Officials came and measured up the available common and woodland, strip arable and waste, and apportioned it among the larger and smaller holders—not equally, but on the principle that "to him that hath shall be given, and he shall have abundantly." Two results followed, the larger holders benefited by acquiring absolute rights over much formerly common land, and the smaller holders found, too late, that they were losing more than they gained. For whereas the big farmer, receiving many acres, ploughed and sowed them with the wheat which at the time was selling at a government-fixed profitable price, the cottar found his new bit of soil too small to grow enough food for his family, and having no longer rights of common pasture, could not keep cow, goat or geese as formerly, nor cut faggots or peat for firing. Moreover, the law said he must fence his holding within a given time, or lose it, and often he had no money to buy fencing. In a few years after 'enclosure' began, thousands of peasants' families, previously self-supporting, were reduced to beggary by the system. Deprived of their old means of living they sought employment on the land of the bigger farmers; if this failed them they were faced with starvation, and could but tramp and beg their way to the towns in search of any kind of occupation which might gain them a wage.

Nor were these dispossessed peasants the only class of countrymen deprived, at this time, of their former means of living. In 1750 wool was still being spun exclusively with the spindle or spinning wheel found in nearly every farm-house and decent cottage. The process of spinning was at best a slow one, and the demand for spun yarn was constant, so all country-women could earn a little money by spinning for the weavers' agents who came to collect yarn for the looms. In 1764 the spinning-jenny was invented by a working weaver, JAMES HARGREAVES; it enabled one spinster to control at the same time eight spindles. Twenty-one years later steam power was applied to this machine, and upwards of one hundred spindles spun wool or cotton simultaneously, thus producing in one place and on one day as much yarn as might have been collected in several days from a hundred cottage workers. Weavers ceased to employ the spinster with her wheel; the owners of the jennies could supply much more yarn for the same wage. The out-of-date spinning wheels were pushed into attic corners to rust, and the spinsters joined the moneyless poor. So also did the carders, shearers, bleachers and dyers—the hand-work of all these artisans was superseded by processes of machine labour before the end of the 18th century.

The first people to experiment with the inventors' steam engines were the capitalist employers of hand labour. Quickly they realised that steam driven machinery would increase the output of their factories; if they could ensure a corresponding increase of sales they might double and treble their total profits. Britain, with its large indigent population and its relatively small wealthy class of land-holders and money-lenders could not provide the market they wanted—but the world was before them, a world without competing machinery. Besides these capitalists there were intelligent and far-sighted artisans and craftsmen who also saw the great possibilities opened up by the steam engine. They scraped and saved to buy one; if individually unable to raise the money they would pool their savings and buy—or it might be they would interest a banker in the venture, and he would lend them part of the price. They would house the steam spindle or power-loom in a roughly-built shed, work day and night to keep the machine busy and extend their custom. Some failed; but the successful repaid their loans and borrowed bigger amounts for the purchase of more machinery and larger premises. Then they began to employ helpers—

but at the lowest possible wage. If children could do the job required they would employ children in preference to adults, because poverty-stricken parents would send their little ones to work for two-pence or threepence a day.

The new steam-engines demanded fuel and water. Coal had hitherto been burned on the hearth in the neighbourhood of the shallow pits, but scarcely at all in furnaces. Until the 18th century wood charcoal was regarded as essential for the smelting of iron, and as the iron industry grew, the forests shrank. In 1735 *coke* was first used for this purpose, and its value as a smelting agent ultimately put an end to the use of wood furnaces. The blast furnace, with its tall chimney, took their place. About 1760 pistons and cylinders began to supersede leathern bellows for draught-making, and after 1783 the steam-engine worked the pistons. The red nozzles of high-pointing furnace chimneys fouled the purity of heaven, belching out heavy smoke which transformed the manufacturing area from a pleasant agricultural region to a 'black country.' The demand of the factory owners for coal grew by leaps and bounds, and so did that for iron ore.

There was plenty of both minerals for the digging. Land-holders prospected upon the estates which had yielded them surface wealth of grain, fruit, wood, and pasturage; and finding coal or iron beneath, began to sink mines. With steam pumps working to drain the water from lower levels the miners were able to delve deeper. But the deeper they went the greater was the danger from 'fire-damp'—the gas released from the coal face, which exploded if brought into contact with a light. To lessen this danger, small doors were constructed at short intervals along the 'galleries'—doors to be opened only when men and trucks passed to and fro. The care of these doors was entrusted to child workers of from five to eight years, who were compelled to sit twelve hours a day in the dark, ready to open the 'traps' when called upon. Children were also employed to fill the small trucks with hewn coal, and bending down or crawling, to drag the trucks through the galleries to the shaft. In an earlier chapter we noted the fate of the slaves doomed to the Athenian silver mines in the 5th century before Christ. Between their lot and that of the small British slaves of the 18th and earlier 19th centuries there was indeed little to choose. Many of the latter were pauper children, sent in batches to mine or factory from city workhouses, who never received a penny for their services. Theirs was labour at its cheapest—upon terms known only to the works' manager and the superintendent of the workhouse. Mine and factory owners, almost without exception, ignored the conditions under which their wretched wage-slaves toiled for them. They thought in terms of tons of coal and iron, of thousands of bales of cotton and woollen cloth, its quantity and sale increasing every year. So did the British government of the time; its attitude is shown by the passing of the Combination Laws. Workmen holding any kind of meeting or 'combining' together to ask for an increase of wages were made liable to a term of imprisonment.

The second half of the 18th century saw the British cotton industry firmly established in Lancashire. Previously it had been discouraged by governments favouring the trade in woollen cloth, which it was imagined would decrease if people got used to wearing cotton garments. In 1720 the use of calico was actually forbidden. But after 1760 there came a change, and we find numbers of cotton 'mills' being started in a small way by Lancashire spinners and weavers. From the first these new capitalists used the improved methods, the lately invented steam-driven jennies and looms, and before long they built up a large British and foreign trade in cotton cloth. During the seventy years after

1763 the imports of raw cotton to Lancashire rose from three million to three hundred million pounds.

. . . .

. . . A new concentration on the production of more real wealth . . . On the large, enclosed farms, improved hand machines for drilling and winnowing; horse drawn ploughs, mowing and reaping machines; the hum of the threshing machine replacing the dull thud of the flails. The sowing of carefully selected seed in deeply ploughed, well-manured soil; the cultivation of root and vegetable crops in frequently weeded rows—such crops providing all-winter food for man and beast. The breeding of sheep and cattle from selected, healthy stock, pasture-fed in summer, but housed in dry stalls during the winter; the consequent increase in quantity of milk, meat, manure, hides and tallow.

Beneath the smoke-clouded skies of the new manufacturing centres of northern Britain and the Midlands a rising hum of driven belts and wheels. More coal, more iron, more and better steel implements. In 1784 the first iron bridge. Ever more bales of cotton and woollen cloth loaded on to waggons and barges, going to the ports, going to London, going to Europe. More clothing of all kinds, more furniture, more ships to bring raw materials into this country and to carry manufactured goods abroad.

Was there more money to facilitate the exchange of this new wealth? All through the century the number of bank-notes in circulation gradually increased. The Bank of England Company and various banking firms in the provincial towns printed these promises to pay gold on demand, and lent them to customers at interest. As long as the banker's credit was good—that is to say, while customers felt sure that they *could* exchange the notes for gold and silver if they wished—the notes continued to serve exactly the same purpose as coin. Buyers would tender them and sellers accept them. Indeed their lightness and the ease with which they could be carried in the pocket made them more convenient than coin, so that holders were ordinarily in no hurry to cash them. Bankers found it safe to issue several times as many notes promising to pay coin as they had coins to pay with. Only when something happened to cast a doubt on a bank's 'solvency'—its capacity to redeem its promises—did people run to its counters demanding coin for their notes. Then, with an excited crowd pressing at his doors, with his cash in hand dwindling fast, the banker was in desperate straits unless he could depend upon large loans from other men of his own profession.

Apart from the risk of a 'run' the trade in money was never more profitable. Few of the enterprising industrialists, who saw the possibility of wealth and fortune in the use of steam power, possessed money for the purchase of machines and the building of factory sheds. Bankers who would lend notes in return for interest, holding the deeds of the factory premises as security, appeared in the light of benefactors. Thus the paper money played its part in assisting the increase of the new *real* wealth of materials and goods; but the interest charges and the eventual obligation to repay the borrowed money added to the prices of the things produced.

Against the general increase of productivity was set the destruction caused by the wars of the period. They were waged, as we have noticed, in Europe, Asia, America, and on the sea. First in order came the Seven Years' War. It was the outcome of a scramble between the French and the British for fresh territory in the New World, and of the land-hunger shown by the Prussian king, FREDERICK the Great, in Europe. We are only concerned now with its economic effect on the people of our own country. As a result of it Canada became a British dominion, and the British East India Company gained much power in India. To pay the expenses of the war, the British government borrowed money from the Bank of England Company and from private lenders, until the National Debt amounted to one hundred and thirty-five million pounds.

On every pound of this sum it was necessary for the government to pay interest annually, so new taxes were imposed, not only on the people of Britain, but also on the colonists of North America. The colonists refused to entertain these taxes, and the British government sent out troops intended to overawe the rebels. Out of these conditions arose the American War of Independence, which ended in victory for the colonists and the consequent foundation of the United States of America.

When that fine statesman, WILLIAM PITT the YOUNGER, came into office he found a National Debt which had risen to the sum of two hundred and fifty million pounds. This meant that a money-lending or *investing* class of persons, representing a small part of the nation, was receiving and would receive in future as interest, much money drawn by taxation from the whole people. The poorer classes were increasing in number, especially where the ugly towns of cheap dwellings were growing round the new factories and mines—since child labour was in such demand, a man and wife, workless themselves, could be kept from starvation by an employed family of children. These poor creatures did not pay direct taxes; they could not; but most of the wretched food they lived on was raised in price by customs or excise duties. Pitt determined to make an attempt to pay off the National Debt; he arranged to set aside one million pounds a year from revenue for that purpose, and might have succeeded in his endeavour had he been able to keep the nation at peace with its neighbours.

Unfortunately there was much ill-feeling against the French in this country; the events of the French Revolution increased this, and war was again declared in 1792. All the industries providing war equipment got busy on urgency government contracts at high prices. The poorer, non-industrial nations of Prussia and Austria, wanted subsidies from the British government in order to buy war materials from British factories. Pitt was obliged to produce more money than taxes would yield. He might have issued paper notes which were government promises to pay coin in due time—but this would have alienated the money-lenders, the wealthiest and therefore most powerful of his supporters. He therefore began to borrow from the Bank of England Company, and in five years had borrowed £90,000,000. Much of this was in gold and silver, which went across to Europe in payment of subsidies. The governor and corporation of the Bank became uneasy, knowing that the possible threat of a French invasion might cause a London panic and consequent 'run' on the Bank by its customers. Pitt agreed that this must be prevented, and accordingly an act of parliament was passed making it no longer compulsory for bank-notes to be exchanged for coin. Except for the payment of soldiers and sailors the bank-notes were to be regarded as *legal tender* throughout the country.

Said a satirist of the time:

"*Of Augustus and Rome*
The Poets still warble
How he found it of brick
And left it of marble.
So of Pitt and of England
Men say without vapour
That he found it of gold
And left it of paper."

What were the general results of this policy? A large proportion of the government's borrowed money went to the industrialists providing food, clothing, transport and munitions for the armies; these providers made high profits and increased their wealth. The stock of available goods and commodities was depleted by excessive war-time consumption, and therefore fewer goods could be marketed. More money, fewer goods—inevitably prices rose. But wages scarcely rose at all, although the cost of provisions nearly doubled.

CHAPTER II

THE INDUSTRIAL REVOLUTION

THE title of our chapter is the term generally applied to the change-over from a general practice of handicrafts in industry to a system of manufacture by the aid of steam-driven machines. It began, as we have seen, in England, about the year 1783; it continued throughout the first half of the 19th century. So much every history of modern times tells us; but many histories pass over in silence other changes, equally revolutionary, which were quietly taking place at the same period and in connexion with the development of power machinery.

Let us make a mental picture of the economic world in which Watt's little steam pump began to work. It was a world of continents and races remote one from another, the only means of communication by land being the horse post, or camel caravan, the canal barge, and by sea the slow, uncertain sailing ship. To most Englishmen or Frenchmen, China and India were still barbaric foreign lands vaguely realised, from whence at long intervals cargoes of tea and spices romantically appeared. The majority of the Chinese and Hindoos had never seen a white man, and knew nothing of European products. Except near the coasts, Africa's dark-skinned millions lived their tribal lives untouched by what we call civilisation. There were Turks in Egypt, and a Dutch settlement at the Cape of Good Hope, but the European's contact with the African villagers was chiefly that of the slave raider. North America, colonised about the lower course of the St. Lawrence and on its eastern slope, was otherwise primeval prairie and forest, yielding only the Indian product of furs. South America hid, in its tropical forests, the remains of a once flourishing, but departed, Indian civilisation; and supported on the north-east a mixed population of Portuguese, Spaniards and half-castes. Australia, visited by Captain Cook in 1770, was known to westerners only as a convict settlement—a remote, savage island on the other side of the world, where undesirables could be dumped with the practical certainty that they would never make their way back again.

Europe comprised a number of big and little states, mostly ruled by princes who kept standing armies and were supported by land-holders of noble rank and the wealthier merchants. A large population of poor peasants and artisans laboured on the land and in the cities. The states were obliged to be mainly self-supporting because of the difficulties placed in the way of trade. Princes, land-holders, town authorities—all imposed duties on merchandise—there was a toll to pay at every bridge or ford, so imported goods were scarce and dear. Each government fortified the boundaries of its territory, and kept a jealous and suspicious eye on its neighbours. The fear of war was never very far away from the minds of the people; and when a quarrel broke out between two of the more powerful states, such as France and Prussia, it was very difficult for the smaller and weaker ones not to be drawn into the fighting.

We should remember:

1. That in 1783 the greater part of the earth's surface was still uncultivated soil—forest, savannah, scrub waste, prairie and desert.

2. That economic freedom, and leisure, were the possession of the few—the majority of the earth's population living in servitude and poverty.

Scarcity and hardship were the lot of the European peasants and middle classes generally; but by rich and poor alike these conditions were accepted as a matter of course. Only in France a group of thinkers, VOLTAIRE and ROUSSEAU among them, had begun to suggest in their writings, plays and speeches, that *freedom* should be the right of every man. It amused the French leisured class to discuss these ideas; and soon the ideal of freedom was communicated to the poorer classes—not intentionally, but because ideas cannot be shut up in any one section of society. The outcome of this was the French Revolution, and the disappearance from France of royalty and the privileged classes.

It is usually easier to pull down than to build up. The ruins of the burnt chateaux might make homes for bats and owls, but not for human beings, and the activities of the guillotine did not provide the starving thousands in Paris with food or clothing. If at this point in their history the French people had been able to concentrate on the re-organisation of production and trade within their own country, the subsequent course of events in Europe might have led more speedily towards economic freedom. But being threatened with war by the governments of the other European states—who had no wish for revolutionary ideas to spread to their own peasantry—all the energy of France consolidated itself for defence and defiance. The cry to arms drowned the cry for bread. By the peasant armies of France should the European peasant brother be freed from the oppression of royalty and nobility! Manifestos were issued inciting the people of other states to rebellion and promising military assistance. Thus began the Wars of the French Revolution, fought in the name of liberty—and resulting, as far as the French were concerned, in their ultimate complete subordination to military dictatorship, and the dominance of NAPOLEON BONAPARTE. Resulting otherwise in unique opportunity for British industries as reconstructed on the lines of steam power and sweated labour.

Since the days of the Plantagenet kings and their establishment of the export trade in woollen cloth the governing classes of England had held fixed principles for the regulation of foreign trade. These principles insisted (a) that it was desirable and necessary to *export* more *material wealth* (especially in the form of manufactured goods) than was *imported*; and (b) that the index of the nation's prosperity was shown by the rise or fall in the amount of *money* received within any given period by British merchants from foreigners. This meant that the nation's prosperity was gauged not by the condition of its people as a whole, but by the money incomes of its masters of production and commerce. So gauged, the period 1792-1815 was one of progress; but a reading of the social history of those years shows a terrible drop in the standard of living generally.

The challenge of the French citizen armies was taken up by the land-holding, royalty-supporting classes of the other European states. The war that began in 1792, and developed later into the wars of Napoleon's ambitions, gave the British farmers and capitalists a fine chance of amassing wealth. Steam power was at home in Britain; but as long as the war went on there would be little possibility of the new processes being set up in Europe. And in the meanwhile the holding up of normal European industries, and the wastage of war, quickened the demand in Europe for British goods. The orders placed with British manufacturers for cotton and woollen cloth, fire-arms, iron and steel manufactures and coal steadily increased. British imports necessarily rose as well as exports, for much raw material used in the factories had to be obtained from abroad. Statistics show that in 1790 the value of exported goods stood at about eighteen million pounds, and that of imports at sixteen millions. By 1815, the final year of the war, the figures were fifty millions and thirty-four millions respectively. An indication of Britain's increasing total of *monetary* wealth is provided by the income tax returns. An income tax[1] of 2s. in the pound, levied in 1799, brought to the government a sum of £6,200,000; in 1813 the same rate of tax realised £14,485,000.

There was also a growing demand for the new, cheap, machine-made British manufactures in the young nation of the United States of America. The former colonists, having succeeded in gaining national independence, were going right ahead to explore and develop the resources of their great country from the Atlantic to the Pacific coasts. As long as their activities were mainly agricultural, while there was rich virgin soil to be cultivated, and homesteads needed building upon new clearings, they would want the British manufacturer to send out ploughs and other farming implements, clothing, and miscellaneous goods for domestic use.

And now, what were these far-reaching changes in life and living, heralded by the little steam pump, and spreading, during the course of the 19th century, from this country outwards, till they affected all the races of the world?

Firstly there was the complete change over from a *feudal* to a *capitalist* order of society—which sounds complicated, but is really quite easy to understand. We have seen (Part I, Chap. V) how in the days of the feudal system everyone but the king himself had a master, a liege lord, or a superior, from whom he received certain rights and benefits whereby he lived, in return for service rendered. Between king and noble, knight and squire, master and man, there were common interests and mutual obligations. The latter were not always faithfully observed, but it was to the advantage of both parties to keep faith one with the other. These

[1]See Note.

feudal ideals persisted through the Middle Ages and into Tudor times. We see them reflected in the Church rubric, expressed in the relationship between masters and apprentices, in those of the Tudor land-holders to their tenants, and in the Elizabethan laws which aimed at keeping the different classes of society each in its place, and at fixing what the government regarded as reasonable wage for work done.

The *capitalist* employer of labour (we have introduced him in Part I, Chap. VII) was, from the 15th century onwards, opposed to any government interference in the matter of wage or price fixing, or any assumption of mutual obligations between himself and his employees. He acknowledged no master. Life for him was a great competition with the other producers of his kind for what he called 'success.' Success meant an increasing number of orders, quick sales, and a big aggregate profit whereby he became monetarily rich. In this competition he gained a point over other producers if he could sell his product a shilling or so cheaper per bale or load than they, for, qualities being even, the retailer would certainly order at the cheapest price. But he could only sell cheaply if his costs of production were low, and so the aim of the capitalist producers, one and all, was to pay as little as possible for raw materials and labour. Their motto was, "*Buy in the cheapest market and sell, as far as you can, in the dearest!*" When the time came, as it did in the late 18th century, that the government of Britain accepted these ideals and framed its policy and legislation with a view to assisting capitalist organisation and benefiting capitalist producers, we may conclude that the capitalist order of society was established. Thereafter the power and energy of the nation concentrates upon the production of goods for *sale*; and since the home population is too poor to buy more than a small proportion of the goods, *chiefly for sale abroad.* A new class of employee, the commercial traveller, begins to function. Commercial travellers, good linguists with plausible tongues, men having tact, push and determination, tour the globe, elbowing their way into palaces, courts and council-rooms, thrusting forward on every available opportunity the names and various products of the firms employing them. Getting orders, orders, the world over, persuading princes, statesmen, pioneers, merchants of all nations, to buy; pitting their intelligence one against another to secure orders. Securing too, raw material at its cheapest; scouring the earth for cheap cotton, rubber, metals—whatever the factories of their firms require.

The unit of feudal society was the small self-supporting community centred round the demesne of the baron; a mainly agricultural group. But the unit of capitalist society was the industrial town. The opening of a new mine, or the building of a factory in a favourable position in respect both of water supply and easy transport to the coast, brought at once an influx of 'hands' to the spot. Rows of cheap, cramped cottages, built by mine or factory owners, housed them. Shops and beer-houses to supply coarse food and cheap beer opened, a few more decent dwellings for managers and foremen arose—and the nucleus of the industrial town was in being. The chances were that other factories would follow; and as long as foreign demand for their produce continued to increase, the 'works' would be from time to time extended, and the town continue to grow. Smoke-blackened, unlighted, unpaved and improperly drained, these centres were dismal abodes of the extremest poverty in the early 19th century. Later on, when the wealth of the owners was established, the more public-spirited of them made efforts to improve the condition of the neighbourhood. Companies were formed to provide a sanitary system and gas (the latter had been invented by MURDOCH of Birmingham in 1797) and some time after 1830 came the railway and railway-station. The employees' standard of living rose a little, though never in proportion to that of the industrialists; and we find that descendants of the original capitalists, men of university education and leisure, sometimes exerted themselves to provide a measure of education for the townspeople, to serve on municipal councils or to assist the construction of public buildings. Meanwhile the population continued to increase.

The ancient city-state and the medieval city could, by careful management, live on the produce of the surrounding farms, supplemented by an import of corn. We have seen with what care the Athenians ensured their supply of grain. But the fast-growing industrial cities of the 19th century soon exceeded the capacity of the surrounding countryside to feed them. Indeed, their growth was itself as dependent upon the provision of a continually increasing supply of foreign food, as upon consignments of raw material. More food—better and cheaper food—was the demand of the cities. And just as the individual capitalist enterprise of the later 18th century saw how, by utilising steam power, it could broadcast the world with manufactured goods and thereby enrich itself, individual capitalist enterprise of the 19th century realised its opportunity in this need of the growing cities for food. The prairies should be ploughed with machine ploughs, and sown with grain. Cattle by thousands should be bred on the grass lands of South America, and sheep by millions on the Australian hills. Fruit should be grown not by the acre, but by the square mile. So the advance of food production began and accelerated, and always the enterprising capitalist received his profit in pounds and the wage-earning labourer his pittance in pence.

Yet how, without a revolutionised *transport system*, could these things have been done? Something faster than the horse, something more commodious than the wagon, was needed. The 18th century solution to the transport problem was the canal barge. The rivers should be linked together by canals, to make an uninterrupted series of water-ways through the country. A great engineer, JAMES BRINDLEY, thus joined the Mersey, the Severn, the Trent and the Thames. The single barge would carry more than many wagon loads, and canal traffic proved much cheaper than road traffic in days when travellers and merchandise were compelled to pay toll at every turnpike gate. But the disadvantage of the canal barge was its slowness, and the canals were deserted after the coming of the railways. . . . Between RICHARD TREVITHICK'S first locomotive, trundling along the highway to the terror of the toll-keeper, and GEORGE STEPHENSON'S railway engine, stretched twenty-eight years of intermittent experiment. Another twenty years, and all the principal British towns are linked to the ports by good railroads and a frequent service of trains. The British ports are brought nearer in point of time to those of Europe and the world in general by the invention of the steam-driven iron ship, the first being built in 1843 by BRUNEL, of Bristol.

The pass-words into this Age of Plenty are therefore *increase* and *acceleration*. More people, more goods and commodities, more money, more opportunities. A speeding up of production and transport. But hampering the course of progress a money system based on usury and the making of undue profit, which dooms the greater part of society to poverty.

CHAPTER III

SOME ECONOMIC THEORIES AND THEORISTS

ECONOMIC freedom for all, as we envisage it to-day, would have seemed to our forefathers of the Industrial Revolution a fantastic and unrealisable dream.

Each of us is born into a world of Things, ready for our use. We spend our early years in learning to use these Things to the best advantage. Later on we discard many of them as old-fashioned, clumsy, and of little value to us, and replace them by others shown by experiment and observation to be more useful and convenient. Similarly are we born into a world of Ideas. These seemed to the generation of our parents wise and incontrovertible, and in childhood we were expected to accept them without question. Some of us, with less discrimination than we show in our judgment of Things, retain these inherited Ideas without testing their truth and value in the light of our own observation and experience. And to do this is both foolish and dangerous, for Life moves on, and Knowledge grows; and the idea which yesterday appeared to be the embodiment of truth may, in the brighter light of to-day, show as a half-truth only, or even as a falsehood.

Consider, for example, the terms *riches* and *poverty!* In the Age of Scarcity it was generally assumed that they expressed conditions of living fundamental in every human community. Charitable persons would make contributions towards the alleviation of the worst suffering of the poor, but they made neither inquiry into the nature of poverty nor experiment with a view to abolishing it, because they regarded it as the inevitable lot of the majority. We know now that poverty is not a natural condition, or a kind of mystic doom afflicting the masses —it is merely a shortage of goods. Moreover, since we are in an Age of Plenty, when electric power is producing not only enough material wealth to supply the need of the entire population, but an increasing surplus, poverty is an artificial and quite unnatural condition.

Our actions are determined by our ideas and our emotions; to understand any course of action we must know the ideas lying behind it. In this chapter we propose to examine some of the chief economic ideas held generally by 19th century people, in order that we may understand their actions, and the development which led the world towards the economic position of the 20th century. We have noted how ideals of individual freedom were sown during the 18th century in France. Contemporary with VOLTAIRE and ROUSSEAU lived a Scotch philosopher, ADAM SMITH, who in 1776 published *An Enquiry into the Nature and Causes of the Wealth of Nations*—a book very widely read and discussed. From this able, and on the whole wise work, two theories passed into the mass of ideas ruling the actions of western communities for the next 150 years. The first was the contention that every man ought to be free to exercise his own powers of initiative, and to make 'the natural effort to better his own condition.' In open, unregulated competition between individual producers of wealth, Adam Smith believed he saw the best opportunity of increase in the quantity and quality of goods, whereby the public, as a whole, would gain; the less the government interfered in the matter, the better! Laws and regulations of the Elizabethan sort, attempting to fix wages and to keep workers to their original trade, or within the parish of their birth, he regarded as being useless and obstructive.

This freely-competitive or *laisser-faire* policy suited the capitalists. They had seen and seized the advantages of steam-power and mass poverty, and wanted to use them to the utmost of their ability. So the British Liberal party came into being, to stand against the Conservative land-holders, to push the interests of Free Trade, the manufacturer and the trader. All through the 19th century we see this idealisation of the competitive spirit. Inasmuch as it gave encouragement to enterprise, stimulating the individual to exert all his powers in the achievement of his aim, it was valuable. But we cannot ignore the fact that it provided an excuse for the most inhuman disregard of the lives and welfare of those whose misfortunes had reduced them to a state of economic servitude.

The second of Adam Smith's theories, which was taken for granted by the 19th century western world, was that relating to *supply and demand.* We have noted how production for *personal and local use* had been superseded by *production for sale.* The modern producer, whether agriculturist or manufacturer, would aim at supplying approximately the quantity of goods for which he could find a market. If he exceeded this quantity, and an unsold surplus of goods remained, that is to say if the *supply* exceeded the *demand*, prices would fall, and instead of making the profit he wanted, the producer would either have his goods left on his hands or would sell them below cost price, and make a loss. Now the governments of the Middle Ages and of Tudor times had resorted to various expedients for regulating the supply of goods, so that the prices of British products should be kept high enough to ensure producers their profits; the argument in favour of this being that fair wages would also be maintained. Such, for instance, as King EDWARD III's prohibition of the export of English wool to Flanders with a view to encouraging the cloth industry at home; the ban on calico in 1720; the

Corn Laws prohibiting or limiting the import of foreign grain until the home supply had become scarce enough to raise farmers' prices above the normal. Adam Smith, perceiving that the effect of these measures was to bring about an artificial scarcity of goods, whereby the whole nation was, as it were, 'rationed' for the benefit of the producers, declared them one and all undesirable. The public demand, said he, should be the only factor regulating supply—and if competition between producers were free and unrestrained, the best foods at the cheapest price would sell in largest quantities, to the mutual benefit of buyers and the more enterprising of the producers.

But in this matter of supply and demand, neither Adam Smith nor any of the economist writers who followed him distinguish between the real, actual need or demand of the populace for food, clothing and shelter, and the *effective* demand of those with money to buy. Tacitly they ignored the greater *real* demand, and dealt only with that fraction of it which the possession of money made effective. Thus, whatever calculations they worked or conclusions they drew could be only partially true, because these were based on the assumption that the total need or demand of the nation was expressed by the total sum of money it spent on goods and services. In concentration upon monetary values these writers lost sight of real values in general. They made no attempt to relate monetary values to actual ones. They wrote, not as economists but as traders, and the subject-matter of their works is better described as commercialese than as economics. Yet, since the trend of 19th century business practice was in line with their theories, these were approved, accepted, and ultimately taught as statements of natural law.

We might summarise points taken for granted by the majority in the 19th century, but which later knowledge is disproving or modern conditions falsifying.

1. The inevitability of poverty.
2. The desirability of free competition in trade.
3. The necessary division of the populace into a minority of potent capitalists and a majority of impotent employees.
4. Great and increasing export trade as evidence of national prosperity.
5. Need for 'favourable balance of trade'—i.e., excess of exports over imports.
6. Leisure as proper only for the wealthy class.
7. The virtue of thrift.

In the case of points 1, 2, and 6, the persuasion of the popular mind was something beyond that of the necessity imposed by the strictly limited total of the world's products. It arose from the religious conviction, "God wills it!" reiterated by the Calvinistic fatalism which took a strange satisfaction in regarding men as working out a fixed and irrevocable doom of happiness or misery. So Christians sang:

> "*The rich man in his castle,*
> *The poor man at its gate,*
> *God made them high or lowly,*
> *And ordered their estate.*"

Although the religious feeling of the time is outside our consideration here, we cannot ignore its expression in this matter. It helped to defeat the efforts of those humanists who, like ROBERT OWEN, saw the condition of the working classes as unnatural and unnecessary.

Of the other writers on what was called 'political economy' (1750-1850) THOMAS MALTHUS was like a raven croaking out the end of the age of scarcity. Writing in 1797 he noted two developments—the increase of material wealth and the unprecedented increase of population. To account for the second he referred to the first, and pronounced it to be a law of nature that the population should always tend to outrun its food supply. Since the increase of food was more than outset by the additional number of children to feed, he thought he need look no further for the cause of the increasing poverty of the masses. This Cambridge don, who had never known want, declared that the poor should be taught to limit the size of their families, to the end that their standard of living should improve—obviously a loaf of bread per day would nourish two children better than six. The closer observation of later observers showed that Malthus was reversing the positions of cause and effect—*when*, and not until the standard of living rose, and workers attained such minimum of comfort and leisure as permitted them to give thought to the planning of their lives, they tended to limit their families to such number of children as they could hope to nurture and educate. It was capitalist industrialism that caused the slum; and it is in the slum that population swarms. The nearer man's condition approximates to that of the beasts, the less power can he exercise in the direction of those instincts common to all life, in the intelligent and perceptive ordering of which lies his human superiority.

DAVID RICARDO, in his *Principles of Political Economy*, published in 1817, accepted the theories of Smith and Malthus. He, also, saw wealth in terms of *money*, and failed to make any useful inquiry into the question of the adequate distribution of real wealth. Instead, he dwelt on the matter of profits and wages. He declared it to be inevitable that, though by continued profit-making the sum of the nation's wealth might be expected to advance, the competition for *work* on the part of the huge masses of wage-earners must keep *wages* at a point near the minimum sum on which existence could be supported. It is no wonder that students of these Industrial Revolution writers nick-named economics 'the dismal science.'

We have mentioned ROBERT OWEN. He was a cloth manufacturer—the outstanding example of a capitalist who did not make Adam Smith's ideal of self-interest the law of his life and business. Instead of paying his employees the minimum wage and wringing from them every possible hour of work he attempted to run his factory at New Lanark with a view to the benefit of the workers as well as to his own benefit. He limited hours of labour and paid reasonable wages. The result of his experiment convinced him that on these lines industry could be profitably run. In 1815 the wars of Napoleon ended and the war-time demand for goods ceased; neither at home nor abroad could British manufacturers find markets for the whole output of factories that had for many years been working on a war-time basis. The surplus goods remained to block up the warehouses; the industrialists turned away thousands of their workers and reduced the wages of the rest; the prices of the unwanted goods went down, and profits also. Sheer starvation threatened the unemployed, although there was no less food in the country than before. Owen saw in this a further proof of the evil of the capitalist system. He began to plan a new one. There was no sense, he maintained, in producing for a foreign market while the very workers who laboured went unfed and ill-clothed. His mind returned to the consideration of the principle of *production for use*. Why should not self-supporting communities be re-established—not on the old feudal lines, but on those of mutual co-operation, each member contributing by his labour to the common stock of wealth, each owning his share in the fixed capital, the factories, machines, tools and appliances whereby the wealth was produced?

This very practically-minded economist wrote essays setting forth his views. They showed his clear understanding of the economic position during the years of national poverty which followed the ending of the war.

> "At the period when peace was last proclaimed, the new powers of supply which had been called into action by the previous extraordinary demand for the materials of war were discovered to be far too abundant for the former peace arrangements of society, founded, as they were, on a profit upon price: and from that period a profit upon price upon the average of all British productions has not been obtained. . . ."
>
> "Since the war ceased production has greatly exceeded consumption, notwithstanding production has been exceedingly restricted in almost all civilised states. *It is not, however, to the interest of any portion of society that production should be restrained, until the wants of all shall have been fully supplied.*"[1]
>
> "The truth is that a profit upon price can be obtained only when the demand is equal to, or exceeds, the supply, while the interest of society requires that the supply should at all times exceed the demand."

Owen was also one of the very few men of his time to realise that the development of power-machinery had inaugurated the Age of Plenty—man's problem henceforth being how best to control and distribute the supply of his abundant material wealth.

> "In the present advanced state of science . . .demand cannot exceed, or be equal to, supply; for a small number of men, with the aid of science properly directed, can easily produce far more than a large number can, advantageously for themselves, consume; the powers of production, aided by science, being almost unlimited."[1]

[1] *An Explanation of the Cause of the Distress which pervades the Civilised Parts of the World.* Robert Owen, (1823.)

Although Owen's theories, backed up as they were by his most evident practical business capacity, commanded attention and respect among disinterested persons, they were naturally discounted and ridiculed by the active and passive supporters of *laisser-faire*. The active ones were those who had thriven, and intended continuing to thrive, by the system; the passive ones the mass of dispirited employees who had been so conditioned by the poverty of their existence as to be incapable of imagining the possibility of economic freedom. The most the latter could hope for seemed to be some amelioration of the worst features of their working conditions, some small wage increase won from the masters by persistent watching of opportunity. The majority, Owen's own workers excepted, looked upon him as a dreamer and visionary.

CHAPTER IV

MONEY IN THE 19TH CENTURY

THE Bank of England Company continued to issue paper money in bank-note form in quantity to suit the requirements of its customers throughout the first ten years of the 19th century. The notes were still promises to pay coin on demand, but since the passing of Pitt's Bank Restriction Act,[1] no one had attempted to exchange them for gold. They cost the banking company very little to make, and the merchants and business men who received them as loans paid interest upon them exactly as if the bank had lent gold.

(There is still a very general ignorance as to the manner in which new money comes into circulation at the present time. Many people think, vaguely, that the Mint has something to do with it. In point of fact, new money starts its career as we have just indicated, in the form of a payment by the banker to his customer; and its supply is regulated in accordance with the demand of bank customers for loans. The Mint is merely the manufactory of coins[2].)

By degrees a certain public discontent with the paper money became evident, and this increased when, at the end of the war (1815) the European demand for British goods fell away, and warehouses remained stocked with commodities none could buy. Producers and financiers were equally concerned. Lowered prices meant lower profits. Few of the industrialists seem to have had any

[1]See Chap. I. [2]See Note.

clear understanding of the situation; many grumbled because there were scarcely any gold coins about, and thought trade might improve if people could again exchange their notes for sovereigns. A Bullion Committee was set up to inquire into the matter. Eventually an Act was passed requiring the Bank of England again to pay coin on demand. In 1826 the one-pound notes were withdrawn from circulation, only those of five pounds value and upwards being retained in use. And since banking facilities were desired in the growing industrial towns of the Midlands and north of England, the founding of country joint stock banks was legalised, these to be at least sixty-five miles away from London. Each new bank issued its own notes, which served as money within the area where the banker was known and trusted.

In 1833 the sixty-five mile limit was abolished, and still more banking companies were formed. These last were not permitted to print and circulate notes. But there had come into use yet another kind of paper money—the *cheque.* The bank-note is the banker's printed promise to pay coin on demand; the cheque is the customer's written request to his banker to pay a stated sum of money to a third person, made on the form supplied by the banker for that purpose.

Cheque money proved to be even more convenient in use than bank-note money, and before the end of the 19th century it was tending to supersede both notes and coin. At the present day cheque money in annual use far exceeds the nominal value of the total coin and note currency in this country. We should therefore clearly understand how cheques function.

Let A. be a cotton manufacturer with an account at B's bank. B. provides A. with a cheque book. When A. wishes to pay C. for goods supplied by the latter, he fills in the appropriate value on a cheque form, signs it, and sends it to C. If C. has confidence in A's integrity

—that is to say, if he has reason to believe A's deposit at the bank is as large or larger than the value stated, he accepts the cheque as payment for the goods.

In the 18th century, when cheques were first used, the recipient probably took his cheque to the bank named upon it, and claimed the sum in question; but this was not the usual procedure later. C. deposits the cheque with his own bank, where its amount is credited to his account; or, alternatively, he may endorse it by writing his signature on the back and pass it on to D. in payment of a debt; in which case D's bank will credit it to D. Thus the cheque serves as money, facilitating the exchange of goods precisely as notes or coin. There is one difference to be observed; by Act of Parliament all Bank of England notes are *legal tender*—the creditor is bound to accept them in payment of debt; this is not the case with cheques.

Joint stock banks played, and still play, a very responsible part in industrial and economic life. The manner in which their business is conducted ought to be common knowledge; but there is, instead, a very common ignorance on the subject, even among those persons who are regular customers at their counters. The composition of the early joint stock banking company was similar to that of joint stock industrial companies; a Board of Management controlled the bank's operations, while the shareholders subscribed the money which formed its capital, and held share-certificates entitling them to *dividends*[1] from profits made. With the capital subscribed the management built or rented business premises, engaged a staff, and printed prospectuses inviting the public to deposit money, and to apply for loans and advances. Two kinds of account the depositor might open with the bank—a *current* account, to the total amount of which (or to any portion of it) he could draw by cheque at any time without notice; and a

[1]See Note.

deposit account, on which the company would pay him interest annually, but which he could not withdraw without giving a number of days' notice.

A sufficient sum having been deposited, the new bank was ready to make 'loans and advances'—for this was by far the more profitable side of its business. Depositor L., we will imagine, is a manufacturer who has to meet a bill for new machinery which will reduce his deposit most uncomfortably—accounts owing to him from customers being overdue. L. applies to the local branch bank manager for an 'advance.' The manager will be delighted to make an advance of, say, £2,000 at 4% (or whatever is the bank rate[1] at the time), re-payable in three months, if L's security is satisfactory. L. produces the title-deeds[2] of a house belonging to him, its approximate value being £2,500, and this the manager accepts, and locks up in his strong-box. The bank ledger is taken down; on the page recording L's account a clerk enters in figures £2,000, exactly as if L. had deposited cash or cheques to that amount; a similar entry is made under the bank's record of loans issued. That is all; the transaction is finished; L. has been 'credited' with £2,000, and he can go home and write a cheque for that amount. The cheque will pay his bill for machinery; the merchant who supplied the machinery will lodge the cheque with his own banker and its sum will be added to his own account. Ultimately L's cheque will be sent to the Clearing House, which is an institution where all cheques deposited at banks are forthwith sent, and where all the amounts owing from one bank to another are balanced up from day to day. A clerk at the Clearing House will subtract the sum of £2,000 from the account of L's bank and add it to that of the merchant's bank.

But what *did* the manager lend L.? Nothing tangible at all. He merely gave L. permission to write a cheque

[1]See Note. [2]See Note.

for £2,000 *over and above the amount of money L. actually held in the bank.* He *created bank credit*[1] in L's favour, and this *bank credit* was entered in the ledger as a deposit in L's name. It is necessary to remember that a large part of the huge sums appearing as 'deposits' on the annually published balance sheets of banks, are not customers' deposits, but bank credit created in this manner—money whose only material form is the 'borrower's' cheque.

L's advance must be repaid in three months' time. Let us see what happens. If he has, by the appointed day, paid in to the bank cheques, notes or coins to the amount of £2,020, the ledger is taken down, the clerk subtracts this figure from L's account, and also £2,000 from the bank's total of 'loans and advances.' The title-deeds of L's house are returned to him, the bank manager records a profit of £20, and the incident is closed. The 'money' with which L. paid for his machinery has gone out of existence. His cheque, its work done, is returned to him, cancelled. It now serves only as a receipt for money paid and received. If, on the contrary, L. cannot repay his advance to date, the bank manager carefully considers his customer's chances of doing so later. If they are promising he may extend the time limit, or offer a further advance on more valuable security; but if he sees little opportunity of retrieving his credit he retains L's title deeds and sells them when occasion offers.

The fore-going illustration should help us to avoid the very common mistake of supposing that bankers and banking firms of the 19th century limited their loans to the amount of the money deposited with them by their customers. Their practice was, and is to-day, to create credit as described, sometimes to eight or nine times the amount of the cash they actually held or hold; in this way serving their customers' temporary convenience,

[1]See Note.

and realising high profits for themselves. The invention of this device of 'credit money' was very important and useful, and the device played a large part in assisting both the increase of material wealth and its distribution, as we shall presently show. The world was indeed furnished with "an imaginary coin to serve the purpose of that which is really so"—in the quaint wording of the 17th century pamphleteer. But, unfortunately, the device was used from the first only in the form of usurious loans, the nature of which were not understood by the general public either in the 19th or in the early 20th century. There are still people at this date (1937) who believe that bankers lend only their own money and deposits entrusted to them by their customers, and who fail to realise that the greater part of the world's money transactions are carried out by the simple process of *writing down figures representing sums of money on cheque forms and in ledgers.*

During the eighteen-thirties there was a 'boom in speculation.' To speculate is to take the risk of losing something—generally money—in the hope of ultimate gain. In the story of Dick Whittington, the merchant, Dick's master, when sending his ship on a trading voyage, invites all the members of his household to add to its cargo some cherished possession which might perchance take the fancy of some foreign prince or trader, and sell for a high price in gold. The ship's voyage was a speculative venture in which *goods* were risked. All through the Age of Scarcity the more adventurous of mankind were ready to risk life and goods to win what was called *fortune*—the possession of a sufficient quantity of money or commodities to ensure economic freedom. After the 17th century speculation generally took the form of buying shares in newly promoted companies promising exceptional dividends. The classic example of this kind of gamble for money is that of the 'boom' of 1720, when the founding of the

South Sea Company fired English imaginations, and extravagant visions of possible profits to be gained by trade with the natives of the Pacific Islands led aristocracy and wealth to rush for the company's shares. In their anxiety to buy them people bid one against another till share certificates certifying an investment of £100 were being sold for £1,000. The appearance of money pouring into the hands of the South Sea Company stimulated clever and unscrupulous persons to float other companies:

> "One was for smelting iron by pit coal; another for 'insuring masters and mistresses against losses caused by the carelessness of servants'; another for 'a wheel for perpetual motion;' and a fourth for carrying on an undertaking of great advantage, but nobody to know what it is."[1]

However unlikely the enterprise, the false confidence and public excitement of the moment ensured it subscribers; and, since prices of shares steadily rose in keeping with the rising demand for them, it was possible to buy one day and sell the next—or even a few hours after buying, and thereby gain thousands of pounds. This went on for some months; then a whisper went round saying that the prices would shortly fall. Everybody who had paid excessive sums tried to sell out quickly, with the result the holders dreaded; soon shares which had been bought for £1,000 could not find buyers at £200, and their owners were left lamenting the fact of a great loss. Many persons of wealth were reduced to extreme poverty.

Nineteenth-century speculation was less crude, but its principle was the same. That axiom of the Age of Scarcity: "It is better to save or invest money than to spend it," was firmly believed and generally acted upon. The more prudent of the poor would stint themselves

[1]Ransome, *History of England.*

week by week of food, clothing and firing, putting regular coppers into savings-box or stocking (where they lay useless for years) in order to 'save up for old age'. Nor were they to be blamed, since no other provision was then made for their sustenance when the wage failed. The middle classes set aside a proportion of their yearly income for investment; the more careful bought shares in Consols (which were Government debt certificates) or in firmly established industrial companies, locked them away in strong-boxes, and allowed the yearly interest on them to accumulate. The more adventurous bought shares at a low price in newer and more risky ventures, trusted to luck or their dealer's foresight that the venture might prosper and prices rise, prepared to sell if the rise occurred; and gained or lost according to the nature of the issue.

Enterprising money-lenders who floated new banking companies between 1826 and 1836 found willing shareholders, for among the gamblers of the 'money-market' the profitable nature of a cleverly run banking business was well known. But unfortunately for the investors, the organisers of these companies were not all cautious enough to secure themselves against the possibility of a sudden drop in public confidence, and the consequent rush of depositors to regain money they thought in danger. The Bank of England Company, backed up as it was by its chief debtor, the British government, and secured by the terms of its charters and its claim on the national taxes, could depend upon the intervention of Parliament in emergency; but this was not the case with any other banking house. Many of these country banks, who had made loans of money and credit to manufacturers, had to close their doors to depositors when their debtors, through failure to sell goods, or other reason, were unable to make repayment. Moreover, banks and industrial firms were becoming interdependent; a bank failure would frequently mean the failure also of the industrialists it financed. In 1837 a large number of banks in the United States stopped payment. English manufacturers, who had supplied the American depositors with goods, were unable to get the money owing to them, and the result was a widespread cessation of trade between the two countries. The Lancashire cotton industry was badly interrupted—in Manchester alone there were 50,000 wage-earners left without employment. Production languished and poverty was rife in this country for the seven succeeding years.

It is essential, in order to understand the way in which production and international trade were extended during the 19th century, to realise that banking companies on the model of the Bank of England Co. ultimately set up business in every European capital, in New York, and in prominent African and Asiatic cities. Further, that producers and merchants ceased to exchange money for goods with one another personally. Each employed the services of a particular bank, drawing cheques and bills of exchange upon it as required, depositing therein cheques and bills received. A cheque paid in and another drawn obviously cancelled each other. At the end of any given period a firm's actual cash in hand could be determined by cancelling its incomings and out-goings. Thus, at the Clearing Houses, where the balances between the banks' accounts were periodically registered, a cheque drawn, for instance, by a customer on Brown's bank and deposited at Smith's bank, would cancel one for a similar amount which had been drawn at Smith's bank by one of his customers and deposited at Brown's; the balancing of the total exchanges would show the monetary position of the two banks in relation to one another. In the case of trade between the merchants of two nations it will be seen that the home and foreign bankers would balance up the values of the bills drawn on either side, and after the cancelling out was done, an *adverse balance* or debt would probably remain

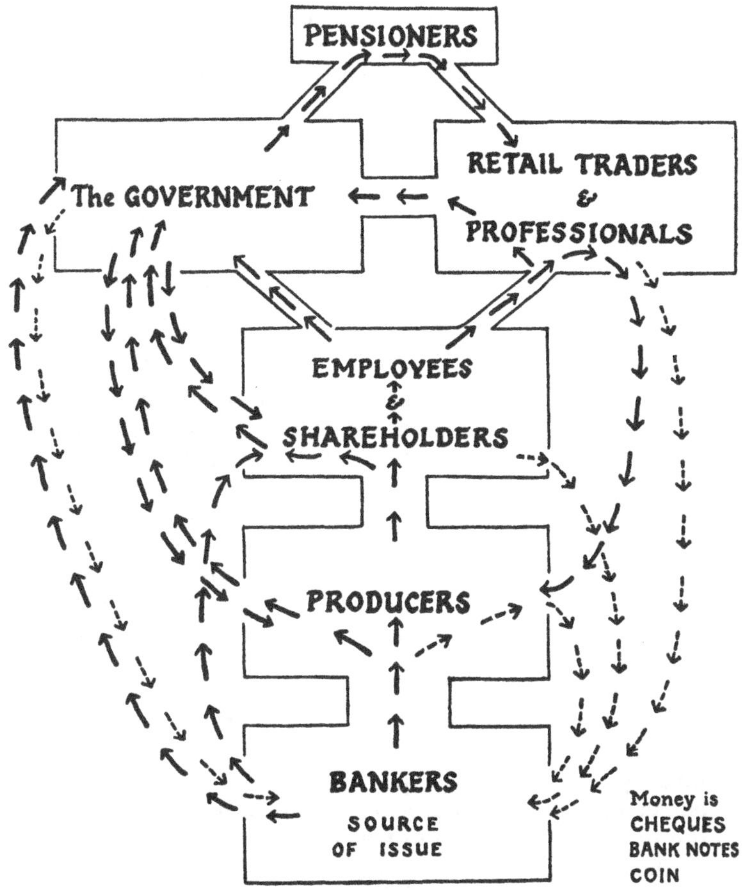

CIRCULATION OF MONEY TO-DAY

owing from one to the other. By international custom such a balance was payable in *gold*. No international paper currency had been devised, acceptable to all nations.

But gold was relatively scarce, and dear.

The banking companies feared what they called 'a drain of gold.'

Therefore they desired their customers, the producers and merchants, always to sell more goods to foreigners than they bought from them; always to *export* more than they *imported*. If the total value of British goods sold to France exceeded in any given period the total value of French goods sold to England, the Bank of France would ship bars of gold to the Bank of England, and the British government acclaim 'a favourable balance of trade.' If the real wealth of the United States came to Britain in excess of the value of manufactures sent in exchange, the Bank of England despatched bars of gold to the Federal Bank of the U.S.A., and the government deplored an adverse trade balance. The index of the nation's prosperity was therefore not reckoned according to the wealth of goods and commodities available for the use of the population, but only according to the bulk of relatively useless metal accumulated in the Bank of England's vaults.

We must note the passing of the *Bank Charter Act of* 1844; since this was a means of regulating and limiting the quantity of money in circulation during the next seventy years. By the provisions of this Act no new banks of issue[1] might be established in England, and the notes of existing country banks were not to be legal tender. Whenever a country bank failed or went out of business the Bank of England Company might increase its own note issue to the extent of two-thirds of the value of the country bank's notes; ultimately, by intention of the Act, the whole note issue should be in

[1]See Note.

the hands of the great bank. And the notes were henceforth to be limited in number; their total face value was to be no more than that of the actual value of the gold and silver held by the Bank, plus an issue of £14 millions worth, called the *fiduciary* issue, which represented the value of securities in the Bank's possession. Theoretically, the face value of the notes in circulation thereafter was to be in proportion to the Bank's stock of coin and bullion. Actually, when a great deal of gold was sent abroad, it was found necessary to suspend this Bank Act, and print more notes, as in 1857 and 1914.

What of the National Debt—that great obligation of the government absorbing in yearly interest so much of the taxes? By the end of the Napoleonic wars (1815) it had reached a total of £860,000,000, and the annual interest amounted to about seventy-five million pounds. If the debt had been divided up among the country's population, every man, woman and child would have owed £43 to the money-lenders. The poverty of the nation during the succeeding twenty years was largely due to the taxation necessary for the gathering of the interest; and the indirect taxes, which raised the price of food and articles in daily use, fell on rich and poor alike. It was estimated that a labourer earning £22 10s. a year had the value of his earnings reduced by nearly one-third in this way.

Many people groaned and protested, but few thought the matter out. DAVID RICARDO was one of the few members of Parliament who probed into the origins of the Debt. In 1824 he published a scheme for the foundation of a Bank which should really belong to the nation as a whole, and not to a private company. The Commissioners or Managers of this Bank, according to Ricardo's scheme, should be appointed by Parliament, and authorised to print national paper money, which should be used to pay off the government's debt to the Bank of England Company. Thereafter, the right of that Company to print notes should be withdrawn, and by degrees the national money be put into circulation, Bank of England notes being received back in exchange for it, and destroyed. The government should also buy gold, either from the Bank of England or from importers of the metal, so that eventually the country would have a debt-free currency, both paper and coin.

Unfortunately, Ricardo died very shortly after formulating his scheme. There was no other economist of his knowledge and experience to support it in face of the opposition it would have been certain to meet from all interested in the profits of private banking. The Bank of England Company's charter was renewed in 1833, and again, as we have seen, in 1844; the National Debt was reduced to some extent during the more prosperous second half of the 19th century, but at no time amounted to less than seven hundred million pounds.

CHAPTER V

THE BRITAIN OF *LAISSER-FAIRE*

BRITAIN, in the 19th century, was very generally known as 'the land of the free.' In song and boast this freedom was glorified. Of what did it consist? In the assurance that as long as the citizen respected the laws relating to life and property, and paid his debts and taxes, the government would not interfere with him. It was conveniently assumed that the citizen had, or ought to have, the means of living; for him to wander 'without visible means of subsistence' was a chargeable offence. In theory every man enjoyed the same measure of freedom. In actuality there was a great difference between the measure enjoyed by the citizen of wealth and that by the landless, moneyless man, the son of the wage earner. For while the former was free to exercise his initiative, energy and ability as and how he would, with materials at his disposal, the latter was compelled to enter an employment in which he could 'earn a living,' whether the employment offered suited his capacities or wasted them.

Nevertheless, in comparison with the other European states, hampered by war or seething with rebellion, Britain was a country of exceptional opportunity. Persons of pluck and energy who could command those two genii Steam-power and Credit-money beheld the markets of the world waiting for their product, while political conditions in Britain assisted and encouraged production. Fertile minds seized upon the problem of transport; and the railway train, which in 1825 had been laughed at as a fantastic and absurd toy, became the indispensable asset of British trade. When the shining metals of the railway track ran from the industrial towns to the ports, and the grooved wheels of engine and trucks glided at the hitherto unknown speed of forty miles per hour, the day of slow traffic on canals was over, and the horse-dray, wagon and coach were retained only for short-distance journeys. But the railways were not laid down to any general plan, with a view to achieving their greatest use and benefit. There was no consultation among the promoters of railway schemes in different counties. They were locally-minded, and their intentions went no further than the attempt to assist local producers and branches of local trade. Dozens of small railway systems were contrived, each the property of a small railway company whose shareholders were usually the local industrialists and traders.

> "As early as 1820 Thomas Grey urged that the matter should be planned and controlled from a national standpoint, and a system linking the big towns and radiating in six great trunk lines from London devised, but he was laughed at as a visionary. So, by 1844, the average length of the railways planned was fifteen miles."[1]

Travel and transport over long distances was at first greatly hampered by the transfers necessary between the systems. The local companies, each jealous of its own trading rights, would not assist one another. Later, however, they began to see that by obstructing traffic they were acting contrary to their own interests, and then amalgamations of the companies took place. When the Great Western Railway Company was formed, controlling 2,993 miles of track formerly the property of 115 small companies, the public and commerce benefited by the institution of a faster and better service,

[1]C. M. Waters, *An Economic History of England.*

much more traffic was handled, and larger profits gratified the shareholders.

In three ways the action of Parliament interfered in the development of the railways, and this may be said to mark the beginning of the movement away from the government's policy of *laisser-faire*. The lines constructed by rival companies were not to be laid so that one obstructed another; tracks had to conform to a high standard of solidarity and reliability; and cheap travel was to be provided for employees and the poor—at least one train per day, stopping at each station on the route, was to carry third-class passengers at the rate of one penny per mile. (1844.)

Public opposition to the railways, which had been fanatical in 1825-30, collapsed entirely between 1840 and 1850. Before the end of the latter year more than 7,000 miles of track were under construction or in plan, and 200,000 navvies were at work, levelling, tunnelling, building viaducts and bridges, laying metals. All the workers were paid wages out of the money accumulated by the new companies—the investments of shareholders and the banks: the navvies at once exchanged their wages for food, drink, tobacco, clothing, etc., thus increasing retail trade within the country. The 'hungry forties' gave place to the more hopeful fifties.

In 1851 the first British Industrial Exhibition, organised by the Prince Consort with the backing of the industrialists, brought British products and engineering prominently before the notice of other nations. This Great Exhibition, in its Crystal Palace of glass and iron, was a forecast of the ideals which dominated the minds of British people for the succeeding eighty years. It was a shrine to the goddess *Foreign Trade*, whose priesthood was the class of financiers and producers who swayed the policies of Parliament and the Cabinet. Except for a minority of land-owners who lived by agriculture, and who opposed the free entry of foreign corn to the country lest their profits on home-grown produce should be reduced, the whole population may be said to have done lip-service at least to Foreign Trade. Everyone agreed that by the gate of Foreign Trade, Prosperity entered. Prosperity meant rising profits and increasing dividends for shareholders; full time—even over-time—labour for the millions of wage earners. It meant more local trade, because increasing wages, salaries and dividends provided more effective demand for the necessities and comforts, the services and amenities of life. "See," said the British industrialists to the world, "with what we can provide you, if you will give us your orders."

The orders came—for railway tracks, rolling-stock, engineering skill, coal, iron and textile goods. In the fifties steam-power was still in its infancy in Europe, where international and civil war, rebellion and revolution continued to hamper invention and production. The French were mining little coal or iron, the Germans and Italians had few factories, the rest of Europe was mainly agricultural. The Civil War in the United States of America (1860-65) brought demands from America for British goods. In the far East, Chinese and Japanese opened (under compulsion) their ports to Western trade.

> "From 1850 to 1873 Great Britain was the forge of the world, the world's carrier, the world's shipbuilder, the world's banker, the world's workshop, the world's clearing-house, the world's entrepôt. The trade of the world during this period pivoted on Great Britain."[1]

Between 1850 and 1870 British contractors built thirty railways in other countries—in France, Italy, Holland, Denmark, Norway, Poland, India, Canada, and the Argentine.

[1] *The Industrial and Commercial Revolutions in Gt. Britain during the 19th Century.* (Knowles).

But this kind of Prosperity brought no *general* increase of leisure or culture. It meant the harnessing of the nation's mental and physical energy to machine production and the organisation necessary for the maintenance of this world-wide commerce.

We have said that the Age of Plenty dawned, unnoticed, with the coming of Steam Power. By 1870 Steam Power had been in operation for nearly a century. What signs of this new age were then visible for all men to see—and what steps towards economic freedom had mankind taken during this century?

Since the British were the first nation to utilise Steam Power we should expect to find these signs most evident in the Britain of the time. There is, indeed, no lack of food for sale; besides home grown produce, imported tea, sugar, coffee, rice, tapioca and other such dry foodstuffs can be bought in town and village shops throughout the land. A great variety of woollen, cotton and silk fabrics, unknown to 17th and 18th century people, and also large stocks of factory-made garments are on sale. All kinds of domestic, commercial, scientific and surgical appliances are obtainable. In the towns buildings have multiplied; the majority are long rows or blocks of uniform dwellings, larger or smaller, put up by landholders or speculative builders for letting to tenants at a profit. Some are more pretentious houses with walled gardens, owned by their occupants, but few have any claim to beauty or great convenience. There are new, ornate, but yet unbeautiful municipal buildings, law courts and council chambers, and a number of new, cheap and ugly schools.

The fish-tail gas flame glimmers in the street lamp; and gas is used for lighting the better class houses. It is made at works belonging to trading companies, who, by arrangement with town councils, convey it to customers through pipes laid under the streets. Municipal authorities are beginning to plan water supply systems, employing engineers to construct reservoirs and install machinery for pumping and conducting the water directly to the taps with which the newer houses are provided. A municipal tax or 'water rate' is charged to owners, and pays for the upkeep of the water supply; but the original cost of the system is generally covered by bankers' loans, the interest on which is added to the town rates. This is also the case with the sewerage systems installed for city drainage. In villages, candles and oil lamps still serve for lighting; water is obtained from springs and wells outside, and often a considerable distance from the dwellings, and sewage is removed by hand-labour.

The standard of life is rising generally. There are many thousands of people living in hovels and slums, doomed to the most abject and terrible poverty, but owing to the demand for labour and the increase of wage-earning, this misery is not so widespread as it was during the period 1815-45. For people in possession of money, never before were there so many opportunities of full and active living, of travel, creative work, discovery, scientific knowledge and fruitful leisure.

As in the ancient, slave-served state of Athens a few leisured Greeks discussed the nature of the system of slavery whereby their personal freedom was assured, so in 19th century Britain a few leisured persons considered the problem of the wage-slave and his poverty. And as the Greeks accepted the slave system, pronouncing it a necessary institution, so the majority of 19th century thinkers regarded the millions of wage-earners as an essential feature of modern civilisation, and their poverty as inevitable. (Nevertheless, fortunate persons not infrequently argued that, if the individual who had been born poor did not 'rise in the world,' it was due to his own incapacity. Grandiloquently the *laisser-faire* enthusiasts pointed to those whose special qualities for the push and thrust of competitive business life had gained them money and power.) There was no public recognition of the passing of the Age of Scarcity; the belief in the inevitability of poverty was shared equally by all classes. Some of the wage-earners looked with hate and envy at the 'idle rich,' and thought that their wealth should be taken away from them and divided among the poor, but more existed in a hopeless apathy, and none would have believed that plenty for all was possible. The dream of WILLIAM MORRIS[1] was for them the vainest of visions. The utmost 19th century wage-earners hoped for was continual work under fairly decent conditions, and perhaps a small increase of wage wrung by hard bargaining from capitalist employers. To this end the more intelligent of them formed Trade Unions.

The Trade Unions were 19th century associations of work-people employed in specific branches of production or trade. Their purpose was rather to maintain the standard of life, to prevent it from being lowered by wage-reduction, than to raise it. The individual wage-earner could do nothing of himself to deter his employer from reducing his wage or from debasing the conditions under which he laboured. If he should refuse to continue working his place could easily be filled by a more submissive employee. But if the whole or any large proportion of the 'hands' employed in a particular branch of industry agreed together to cease work until such grievance were removed the industry was faced with disorganisation and loss of contracts and profits.

The organisers of the Trade Unions aimed first at accumulating by regular subscriptions from members a central fund of money to provide for expenses of organisation, legal advice, and 'strike pay'—a small weekly sum payable to each unemployed member if a strike should be decided upon or the employers declare

[1]*News from Nowhere.*

a 'lock-out.' This fund accumulated, the Union was ready to resist attempts at wage-reduction, or, alternatively, to present a demand for a small increase if conditions seemed to justify it. The *threat* of a possible strike was the force upon which Trade Unionists depended wherewith to coerce their employers; the strike itself they desired to avert. It was a weapon that wounded those using it; the loss of wages could never be outset by the 'strike pay' contributed towards the strikers' expenses from the Union funds; and the depletion of these funds meant the weakening of the whole organisation. The employers would only consider the proposals of the Union if convinced (a) that its funds were large enough to support a protracted stoppage of work, and (b) that they themselves stood to lose more in the long run by such a stoppage than by conceding at least some part of the Union's demands.

Between 1799 and 1824 all Trade Unions and 'combinations' of workmen had been forbidden in England by the *Combination Laws*. These laws had been easily passed through Parliament at the time when the middle and upper classes of English society, the events of the French Revolution fresh in their minds, were roused to suspicion and fear by the least attempt on the part of wage-earners to get together in clubs or associations of a self-help character. But in 1824 these Combination Laws were repealed,[1] and thereafter many Trade Unions were founded from time to time, endured for a longer or shorter period, and (in the case of the earlier ones) disappeared as their supporters realised how little they could accomplish of their declared aims. From 1824 to 1834 the ideals and plans of Robert Owen and his friends kindled the hopes of millions of wage-earners; a Grand Consolidated Trades' Union was formed, workers of all industries being invited to join. They joined; but

[1]The work of two able men, the tailor Francis Place and the politician Joseph Hume.

unsuccessful strikes soon discouraged them, membership fell off, and eventually the Union broke up. The leaders themselves were keenly disappointed; they had failed to realise how the poverty-narrowed lives of the wage-earners prevented all but a few from seeing beyond their own personal advantage; if some immediate satisfaction of personal need were not to be gained, enthusiasm and support for the Union died.

Yet Trade Unionism was not an entire waste of effort. The organisers learned something by their early mistakes, and in later years many concessions were won from capitalists by well-financed unions. Trade Unions kept the case of the wage-earner before the notice of a leisured public which was not without humanitarian feeling; and the gradual rise in the employee's standard of living was partly due to their influence. They belonged properly to an Age of Scarcity which was fast passing away; but of all their devoted and energetic leaders, Robert Owen alone seems to have perceived the reality of the Age of Plenty, and the new state of freedom it made possible for the slaves of industry. "*It has been ascertained*," he wrote in 1823, "*that the new powers of supply*[1] *in Great Britain, derived from science within the last forty years, exceeds the labour of* 350 *millions of adults*." If the estimate to which he referred was excessive in 1823, scientific invention had fully justified it by 1870, and was yet only beginning to show what electric power could achieve in the field of production for man's use.

But 19th century wage-earners found no joy, no happy anticipation of future plenty and freedom in the application of science to industry, and in the steady progress of mechanical invention. To them the machines invading farm and factory seemed enemy powers, come to take from them the work and wage whereby they lived. What mattered it to them that produce increased four-

[1]Steam power and machine invention.

fold—or a hundred-fold! that the world's wealth of necessaries and luxuries was piling up year by year! Their portion of this plenty was measured and limited by the weekly wage, the monthly salary; and the wage, the salary, was payment for labour, not to be obtained except in return for labour. Every labour-saving invention and device, every machine which reduced the number of 'hands' employed in industry naturally took a menacing shape in the eyes of the wage-earner, a shape threatening his very existence.

There had been machine-smashing in the earlier days —before 1780 spinning-jennies were destroyed by displaced workers. After 1802 the gig-mills (machines for raising the nap of woollen cloth, thus superseding the teasels of the *rowers*) were attacked; also the mechanical shearing-frames that rendered the *shearers'* trade obsolete. The Nottinghamshire *Luddites* smashed as many as a thousand hosiery frames in 1812-13, and a few months later mills with power-looms were burned in Lancashire and Cheshire. Again in 1826, when a falling-off in the market demand for cotton cloth reduced the Lancashire weavers to great distress, the power-looms of Blackburn and Bury were destroyed. No permanent advantage to the wage-earners resulted from this sabotage; and the harsh laws of the time imposed the death sentence upon convicted offenders, without regard to the circumstances which had provoked the crime.

As the century advanced the wage-earner's active opposition to the machine lapsed into quiescence. He realised that machines had come to stay, and that no protest he could make would alter that fact. The machines themselves had to be made, and their manufacture employed men—if they took work from some, they gave it to others. The wage-earner hoped the balance was in favour of a bigger total of labour. But still he regarded them as in main the allies of the capitalist, ranged upon his side against the worker.

CHAPTER VI

THE COMING OF ELECTRIC POWER

IN 1831 MICHAEL FARADAY, the Yorkshireman, experimenting with the electric current along lines suggested to him by the study of earlier investigations, discovered the principle of the *dynamo*. His actual experiment is described in his scientific work "*Experimental Researches of Electricity*."

The natural force to which WILLIAM GILBERT had given, in 1600, the name *electrica*, was first observed in connexion with the action of magnets. A long line of investigators succeeded Gilbert, and by the time of Faraday's birth the general character of the electric current, its induction and mode of action, were known. It remained for Faraday to determine how these might be put to practical use. He "laid the foundation for all subsequent inventions which finally led to the production of electro-magnetic or dynamo-electric machines."

Sir HUMPHREY DAVY had shown in 1808 that electric light was a possibility; but not until 1880 did a satisfactory electric lamp make its appearance. Telegraphy was the first practical application of electricity, messages being sent overland at Göttingen in Germany, in 1836. An electric submarine cable from Dover to Calais was laid successfully in 1851. Then in 1856 an Atlantic Telegraph Company was formed, and electricians and engineers applied themselves to the task of laying a cable along the bed of the Atlantic Ocean from Britain to America—the then largest steamship in the world, the *Great Eastern*, was specially built for the purpose. The first cable broke while being laid; the second, though immediately successful, soon snapped; but the work was finished with complete success in 1866.

Steam-power drove the first magneto-electric machines. One of the earliest was used on Dungeness lighthouse in 1862. With 1876 came the invention of the telephone; a telephone exchange made its appearance in the United States in 1879. The Crystal Palace, home of the great industrial exhibition of 1851, housed a British Electrical Exhibition in 1882, and the same year saw a public electric supply station opened as a commercial proposition in Holborn, London. Electric traction dates from about the same time, an electric tram-car being on view in Paris in 1881. Invention of electrical apparatus was in no wise the monopoly of British scientists; Europeans and Americans were equally engaged in research and experiment, and acquired a common fund of knowledge from which the whole world ultimately benefited. Of this honourable company of inventors we may remember a few outstanding names; but it is well to realise that a great bulk of steady, unrecognised scientific work, carried on by hundreds of comparatively unknown investigators and engineers, went to the building of the structure of 20th century electrical achievement. Moreover, no modern machine is a one-man invention; but each machine is the ultimate result of a long sequence of experiment and discovery, and represents the life-work of a long succession of engineers.

Commercial companies were formed with the object of generating a supply of electric power to the public for house and street lighting. But its sale was not so simple a matter as that of food or clothing. Electric power could only be conveyed to buyers by means of fixed standards and wires, or underground cables; and for the placing of these the sanction of the various municipal authorities had to be obtained. Generally speaking, the town councils were not anxious to extend privileges to the commercial companies, and a British Act of Parliament passed in 1882 provided that electric power systems set up by commercial companies should pass, after twenty years, by purchase under the control of the municipalities concerned. Under this condition investors were not eager to buy shares in the companies, and the progress of electric lighting was slow, but six years later the Act was altered to the advantage of the producers, and thereafter the provision of the current went forward more quickly.

Between 1890 and the end of the century electrically propelled trams and trains began to make their appearance in the cities of Europe and America. It was also found that the natural force of swiftly running or falling water, formerly applied to the machinery of water-mills, could be utilised to drive dynamos for the generating of high electric power; the falls of Niagara were thus harnessed, and the electricity provided was transmitted to all the towns and factories within an 18 mile radius. In hundreds of ways electric power was applied to industry. One happy result was, that the smoke nuisance consequent upon the use of coal and coke furnaces essential to steam-power, abated; factories and industrial towns tended to become cleaner and healthier places. This, however, was more noticeable after the first decade of the 20th century, when electric power had been more generally applied to cooking and heating in homes and public buildings.

The new processes connected with the making and running of electrical machinery of all kinds created new trades. A vast number of previously unthought of goods and commodities, from motor cars to electric bells were placed upon the market, and their convenience and use created an immediate and continuous demand for them among the classes of people who had money to buy.

The raw materials—vegetable and mineral oils, rubber, vulcanite, copper, nickel and other lesser known but now indispensable metals—were not all to be found in any one of the industrialised countries. The needs of the industrialists sent their agents prospecting throughout the hitherto unexplored world in search of these valuable products. Bankers and financiers, always with a view to future profit-making, advanced (or even donated) the money to fit out such parties of scientific explorers.

To sum up the results of the application of electric power to the world's production and distribution of natural wealth:

(1) The *rate of production* progressively increased; i.e., each manufactured article took a shorter time to make—or, conversely, more articles could be made in the same time.

(2) Since there was no necessary increase in the time taken to *wear out* an article (this wearing-out process is termed *depreciation*) there was a progressive increase in the total of manufactured goods used; and also a tendency to the accumulation of surplus, unsold goods in warehouses.

(3) The *rate of distribution* also increased. Modern cranes, cars, ships, etc. were continually breaking records for efficiency and speed of delivery. Conversely, an apparent (not actual) decrease in the distance between the source of raw materials, the factories to which they were bound, and the markets, helped to make quick sales essential.

(4) The quantity of *human labour* necessary for production *decreased* progressively. Electrical machines took the place of many wage-earners.

(5) The total amount of money paid out in wages began relatively to decrease.

(6) The number of 'unemployed' men and women began relatively to increase.

CHAPTER VII

THE RACE FOR FOREIGN MARKETS

AND so we approach the economic world of the 20th century. Before entering it, let us take a birds'-eye view, and compare it with the world of a century past, visualised in Chapter II.

The oceans are now dotted with thousands of ships, steaming rapidly from port to port; it is a commonplace to make the voyage from Europe to the Antipodes, from San Francisco to Japan. The majority of ships carry cargoes—grain, fruit, raw materials or manufactured goods. Great liners, equipped like hotels, convey hundreds of passengers each voyage from continent to continent. A minority of ships are simply steel platforms, mounting long-range guns—vessels of destruction.

Europe and North America are threaded by railway systems and good roads. A day and night service of goods and passenger trains links coast with coast and the large cities with the country towns and villages. Telegraph poles march along by railroad and roadway; every village has its post and telegraph office. Look at Asia! it also boasts a railway and telegraph system, though this, as yet, is only partially developed. One line crosses the Ural Mountains and joins Russia with China; several have been laid in India; brown men of the Ganges basin travel by train to Delhi, to Benares, to Calcutta. There is even a railway-engine puffing in remote Japan. In Africa the Egyptian fellaheen is now as well accustomed to the sight of the train as to that of the camel caravan; and the Dutch Boer and Kaffir tribesmen of the South know it also—there it is taking the place of the ox-wagon. Only over the world's more barren and inaccessible deserts, Gobi and the Sahara, and Central Australia, or through the thickest tropical forests of the Congo and the Amazon, there is still no means of steam transport or electric communication.

The raiding of African villages to supply slaves for tropical and sub-tropical plantation work has practically ceased. This kind of blatant slavery became obnoxious to a majority of western nations. The American Civil War (1861-65) turned upon this issue; it was fought between the cotton plantation-owning Southerners and the people of the Northern States; the Northerners won and the negro slaves in all the States were subsequently freed. Domestic slavery, however, persists in Asiatic countries and in the native African states of Abyssinia and Morocco; and there is plantation slavery in the Congo region under Belgian control.

The African continent, where black and brown primitive peoples had maintained through the ages their tribal nomadic or hut village life, has now passed under the administration of the dominant European nations. Exploring expeditions—French, British, German, etc.—have traversed it from north to south and from east to west, the leader of each expedition claiming in the name of his king or government the right of making trading treaties with the native chiefs. There has been much discussion and no little disagreement among Foreign Ministers as to the precise limits and boundaries and 'spheres of influence' recognised by their respective nations. Thousands of natives work on the white traders' coffee, cotton, rubber, cane sugar, tobacco, cacao and banana plantations, or in the gold or diamond mines—thus earning the money to pay the hut tax collected from them. The products of the plantations, and the natural wealth of the tropical forests, are shipped to Europe for manufacture or sale.

North America retains its thick forests only because 'lumbering' is regulated by government. The prairie land of the Middle West is ploughed and sown with wheat; it forms one of the world's greatest grain-producing areas. Many thousands of emigrants, in search of better conditions of living than their native Europe or Asia affords them, are entering Canada and the United States each year. The latter country is now explored from the Atlantic to the Pacific coasts, and all the best agricultural land is under cultivation; vegetable and mineral wealth are enormous, manufactures increasing in bulk and variety. The decisions of the people of the United States in matters relating to production and trade are tremendously important to the world as a whole. South America is less densely populated; its people rear great herds of cattle on the grass lands of the Argentine and export them as meat to Europe; coffee is a staple product; the deserts of Chile yield the nitrates now become essential to supplement Europe's insufficient supply of natural manure.

Eastern and south-eastern Australia are fully colonised; the chief industries here are large-scale sheep-farming, and mining for gold and silver. The larger colonial towns possess all the modern engineering amenities of European cities. It is the same in the islands of New Zealand—pastoral colonies exporting frozen mutton and dairy produce to Britain.

The larger European states have, in their turn, passed through an 'industrial revolution' similar to that of Britain. France and Germany especially have developed great manufactures, drawing their raw materials partly from abroad. And as in Britain, the populations have increased.

Summing up as in Chapter II we note:

(1) That at the beginning of the 20th century, the greater part of the world's best land was under cultivation, and a large part of its mineral wealth was located and in process of being worked.

(2) That the western nations generally had adopted mechanical industrialism, and were producing *goods for sale*.

(3) That dense populations were becoming increasingly dependent on *imported* food.

(4) That economic freedom and leisure were still only possible to a small percentage of the world's people.

We must now look more closely at the most powerful western nations.

Britain, in 1900, supported a large urban population and a small and decreasing rural one. Of the country people, some farmers owned and farmed their own land, more hired their farms from leisured landowners, the rest were wage-earners working on the farms or estates of the land-owners, artisans, employees of local government authorities, or petty tradesmen. Only about a tenth of the producer part of the nation's people was engaged in agriculture and dairying, so not nearly enough food was produced within the country to supply the general need; this was met by colonial and foreign imports. Stacks of foodstuffs were always on sale in the shopping centres, and no small quantity of the perishable varieties remained unsold and was wasted (although it must be remembered that the poorer wage-earners and the unemployed were undernourished because they lacked the means to buy).

The economically independent class owned houses in London and other socially important cities. The majority of townspeople lived in hired houses. All were dependent upon shop supplies for food and clothing, excepting those few who drew dairy-produce, fruit, etc.

from their own country estates. The economically dependent formed the mass of the town population, and these worked for their wage at a more or less mechanical 'job' from the end of their school days to old age, or till physical or mental breakdown ended their working capacity. Yet we note, by comparison between wage-earners' conditions in 1800 and those in 1900, certain steps towards economic freedom. By the latter date the average length of the working day had been considerably shortened, and public opinion had conceded that an annual holiday of at least a week should be allowed the worker. Many of the trading and industrial firms permitted their employees this leave of absence without loss of wage.

The 'visible' exports streaming outwards from Britain were manufactured textiles, light and heavy metal goods, and coal. But British enterprise was also providing 'invisible' exports, in the form of the carrying services rendered to merchants of other nations by shipping, and in that of loans advanced by bankers and others to foreign buyers with a view to increasing the sale abroad of British goods. By 1890 more than two thousand million pounds[1] had been 'loaned' in this way, the annual interest (when it was forthcoming) adding to the incomes of the investors concerned. But it was not so easy to compel interest payments from persons living beyond the jurisdiction of British law, nor was it always possible to sell the securities pledged by such persons, so these foreign investments carried much risk of loss to their holders.

Between 1878 and 1886 British import and export trade slackened. Durable and tenacious steel, made by the Bessemer process, was superseding iron for railway metals, girders, ship construction, etc., and British iron ore was not pure enough to be made into steel. (Suitable ores were later imported from Bilbao and Sweden.)

[1]Prof. A. L. Bowley.

European nations and the United States were beginning to manufacture largely for themselves, and their governments put new import duties (tariffs) on foreign goods in order to raise the prices of such goods above those made at home. The French, defeated in the Franco-German war, were taxed to pay a heavy indemnity to the Germans, and could buy little for their own use.

What was the British producer to do?

We must bear in mind that the majority of industrial concerns were now joint stock companies.[1] Very few firms of the individual or family sort remained—manufactories controlled by owner-proprietors benefiting by all profits made. The manager or *entrepreneur* of the joint stock company's manufactory was a salaried official who held his position at the pleasure of the Board of Directors representing the shareholders. This official might expect a rise of salary if he (a) reduced the running costs of the concern (b) showed an increase of profit at the year's end (c) obtained more orders for the product. It mattered nothing to him whether the goods were sold at home or abroad, who bought or who, for lack of money, went without. He had to concentrate on maintaining prices and increasing profits. He had to *sell.*

When the European and American demand for British goods fell off, it simply did not occur to industrialists that a great population amounting to millions lived in the home country unsupplied or only half supplied with the necessaries of life. It did not seem in the least extraordinary that goods needed in Britain should be hawked in Japan, nor that looms which might have clothed British children should weave cloth for the slaves of an oriental court. "We sell," the industrialists would have said if questioned, "for money. It is no business of ours to inquire why some people have money and more have not." Which was true. It was rather the business of the banks, and especially of the Bank of

[1]See Note.

England, to provide money, to create it as it was needed. And as we have seen in Chapter IV, all the new money issued was in the form of loans at interest, and this was granted only to those with property to pledge in security for the return of the loans.

So the industrialists turned to the British colonies—the lands where emigrants were developing virgin soil granted to them free or at cheap rates by the government; and where mining was going forward under the direction of newly-formed companies. There was much public talk, much writing of books and newspaper articles about a united British Empire—an empire including India, Canada, Australia, New Zealand, British Africa and the various island colonies—which should carry on a reciprocal trade with the 'mother land,' and make the latter independent of customers in 'foreign' countries. At a special ceremony the English queen VICTORIA was declared Empress of India. . . . The bankers and men of the money-market also looked towards the colonies; it was made easy for the emigrant-farmers to borrow money on the security of their farms for the purpose of buying new stock and the latest machinery.

The construction of the Suez Canal, linking the Red Sea with the Mediterranean, was one of the engineering triumphs of the 19th century. A glance at the map will show how greatly the use of this canal shortened the voyage from western Europe to India and the East. The canal's construction was financed by a joint stock company, the majority of the shares belonging originally to the Khedive ISMAIL, ruler of Egypt. This king received large loans from British financiers, spent the money partly on engineering works and partly on local wars, and presently found himself unable to pay his interest in spite of the heavy taxes imposed on his people. He decided to sell his Suez Canal shares; and the British prime minister of the time, Lord BEACONSFIELD, arranged to buy them for his government at a price of £4,000,000. This action placed the control and the revenues of the Canal mainly in British hands. A few years later commissionaires were sent to Egypt in the interests of the Khedive's creditors to inquire what monies he received and how they were being spent; the administration was seen to be bad and wasteful, and eventually Ismail was compelled to abdicate in favour of his young son, whose policy was supervised by British officials. The new king was unpopular in his country; his subjects, mostly Muhammadans, resented the dominance of Christian officials, and the fact that half the taxes they paid went to meet the interest of foreign bondholders. There was a rebellion which a British army quelled, and after 1882 Egypt became a *protectorate* of Britain, and practically under British government.

Meanwhile, the peoples of Europe generally had adopted the industrial and banking systems that originated in Britain. French, Germans, Italians, Belgians, Dutch, all wanted colonies that would provide them with raw materials, world-wide markets for their goods, and borrowers to whom they could loan money. The French acquired great territories in north-west Africa, the Germans tracts of the continent both east and west, the Italians attempted to occupy Abyssinia by force of arms, but were defeated by the native warriors; the Belgians obtained the Congo Free State; the Dutch retained Java. The Japanese archipelago excepted, there was not an islet in any of the oceans unclaimed by a European or American state. British, Germans, French and Russians all went to China eager to gain trading rights and concessions from its weak and decaying government. And the vigorous little nation of Japan was watching keenly, and imitating the methods of the western powers. Japan would borrow and lend, manufacture and sell.

Competition for sales grew ever more fierce.

Most nations, to 'protect' their own industries, put high import duties on 'foreign' goods of the same class, thus raising the retail price of these. For the masses of the people, always short of money, would not buy home-manufactured goods, unless they were cheaper than those imported. Only Britain retained free trade, possible because of this country's vast number of overseas' customers, and desirable because insufficient food was produced in the homeland. Strange measures were taken to undersell competitors. The French government paid a 'bounty' to all French producers of beet sugar for the English market, thus enabling them to sell it in England at a cheaper price than the West Indian cane sugar could be sold. By this means the French hoped to kill the West Indian trade, and capture the English sugar market. So, for years, the French housewife had to pay more for French sugar than did her British neighbour.

Year by year the progress of invention increased the rate of production, but the rate of sale moved much more slowly. Goods piled up in warehouses; firms were compelled to reduce their output and discharge workmen. Even if the machines had been running full time unemployment would have been increasing, for the newer machines were more efficient than those they displaced, and required fewer hands to tend them.

The competing industrialists worked hard to improve the quality of their goods. They appointed salaried horticulturalists of high qualification to superintend the plantations producing their vegetable products, and skilled chemists to experiment with raw material with a view to treating it in the best possible way. Food stuffs became ever more appetising, more varied, purer; clothing materials more attractive and comfortable; furniture and fittings more convenient and artistic. The 'moneyed class' bought only of the best and latest goods; the class without a banking account stared at window shows and bought the cheapest.

Advertising, in the earlier days of the century, had been a mere distribution of hand-bills to city residents, or a postal notification of special goods to country house buyers. Now the great advertisement hoardings appeared; the poor artist found that he could earn by applying his art to commerce, and designing flamboyant posters which compelled the public eye and mind to dwell on the excellence of the advertising firm's soap, or pickles, tobacco or patent medicine. Nearly all journals and magazines admitted advertisements; no one could open a newspaper without being faced with a recommendation to buy goods which either he could not, for his poverty, purchase, or did not want.

But still production exceeded consumption, and unused goods, commodities and services continued to accumulate. We have seen that when the quantity of goods offered for sale considerably exceeds that for which there is an effective demand, prices will be reduced, and that reduced prices mean lowered profits, or perhaps no profit at all, but a loss. Certain large industrial firms, dealing in the same class of commodity, agreed to act together for the purpose of keeping up the price of their product. Instead of competing one against another they decided upon a uniform price, and supplied retailers with the product on the understanding that this should not be lowered. There were also industrial and mercantile amalgamations of the producing joint stock companies; these gigantic concerns, called *Trusts*, were first known in the United States.

With the Trusts, competitive trading began to draw to its end. For they controlled mines, plantations, factories and shops—and in all their hundreds of stores the public paid a uniform price for the goods and commodities supplied.

CHAPTER VIII

THE ECONOMIC SIDE OF THE WORLD WAR

THE breaking out of war among European nations in 1914 surprised the majority of people in this country. Millions of workers, living narrow, laborious lives walled by poverty, knew at the time little more of important events, those affecting the destiny of the world, than the head-lines of their half-penny papers told them. Thousands of persons better off, whose means enabled them to travel, and whose reception abroad had been charming and friendly, wondered exceedingly why, when no enmity appeared to exist between nations in ordinary life, governments should declare war. The governments in question supplied various sentimental reasons which were generally accepted, and modern war—the wholesale destruction of human life and property by explosives manufactured for that purpose—proceeded.

Only those few people who had studied and watched the trend of economic events, the matters connected with international production and trade, really understood the reasons for which the nations were waging war on one another. These saw that the root causes of this terrible and unnatural enmity of governments, that set men with no personal animosity against one another to mutual slaughter, grew out of the muddled ideas and false ideals of 19th century commercialism.

Firstly, there was the *laisser-faire* ideal—that glorification of selfishness which encouraged the individual to advance and enrich himself by any legal means that offered, ignoring completely the consequences to others of his actions. We have seen that the *industrial* working out of this ideal tended towards (1) the impoverishment and subjugation of employees, the continuance, in every industrial country, of a great class of economically unfree and very poor persons; and (2) a minority class of wealthy ones. Its *national* application excused and justified tactics whereby traders of one nation snatched a trading advantage from competitors of another nation.

Next among the root causes of war was the general adoption of the principle of usury throughout international business life. Governments, town councils, industrialists, agriculturalists, colonials, all were in debt to the bankers who had advanced them 'credit' at interest, or to the financiers who had bought from them 'interest-bearing bonds.'[1] This burden of debt, of interest charges to be met annually, weighed heavily on the public mind. It increased taxes, rates, and prices of goods; it accentuated the shortage of money, and brought financial anxiety into the lives of the citizen majority. The principle of usury affected no less the relationships between nations: there were loans outstanding in favour of creditor governments.[2] It was a galling thought to the subjects of Nation A. that they were being taxed to meet the interest charges of Nation B. The position did not assist international good feeling.

Britain's claim to be 'the world's workshop' was all very well when no other nation was equipped to supply necessary industrial goods. But now there were five other large 'workshops,' France, Germany, Italy, the United States, and Japan, besides smaller ones. All these, the United States excepted, needed colonies to provide them with rubber, oil, cotton, and other raw materials. All wanted to sell in foreign markets, the mass of their home populations being short of money.

[1]See Note. [2]See Note.

. . . And Britain's position as 'the world's banker,' creating credit-money for the other nations, could only remain unchallenged until banking companies similar to that of the Bank of England Co. were fully established in Berlin, Paris, and New York. With ALL these 'world's workshops' producing for foreign trade, and ALL these 'world's bankers' trying to make loans abroad, while the majority of people in ALL the western nations were too short of money even to buy a sufficiency of food and clothing—was it surprising that the fierce competition for international trade engendered international irritation and fear! Such fear profited the armament firms and those financing them, since the various governments began to put in additional orders 'for defence.' Each new battleship, submarine, gun of longer range, more deadly torpedo, made for Government A., increased the resentment and apprehension of Governments B., C. or D., so that these hastened to equip themselves similarly, or with some additional armament.

There are two ways only of stopping this kind of race in accumulating engines of destruction. One is by international agreement to disarm; the other is by beginning war. The governments of this first decade of the 20th century were too suspicious and mistrustful of one another to do the first. It could be, therefore, only a matter of time before some government, feeling for the moment a little ahead in the armaments race, or aware of circumstances temporarily hampering its competitors, would declare war. In 1914 the German government took the fatal initiative. The conscript armies of Germany were ordered to march through Belgium into France, to occupy Paris. Germans had gained an easy victory over the French in 1870—it might be repeated. Another heavy war indemnity from France would pay for the expensive new German navy and other armament whose cost was weighting German citizens' taxes. . . . If Britain would not interfere. . . .

But this time the British government did interfere. It had viewed with extreme disfavour the expansion of the German navy, and the immense development of German steel, cotton and chemical industries—now turned to war-time uses. One of the German writers had said that his countrymen wanted 'a place in the sun.' If the French were beaten, and a German government became all-powerful in Europe, it would surely challenge the right of British industrialists to retain the material wealth of so large and profitable a Colonial Empire as that on which 'the sun never set.' . . . The British army was mobilised and sent to the aid of the French.

The Russian monarchy,[1] which had depended much upon French loans, also mobilised its army and attacked the eastern border of Germany. The Austrian monarchy,[2] allied with the German emperor, was already attacking Serbia, on the pretext that the Serbian government had connived at the assassination of an Austrian arch-duke. (This latter incident, a murder committed by an irresponsible young Serbian, was like a match setting fire to a long train of accumulated international bad feeling.) Four years of war ensued, impoverishing the whole of Europe.

A declaration of war is a national determination to destroy—to concentrate the resources of the nation primarily upon destructive purposes. Immediately the war began, destruction began; first to suffer were the Belgian villagers whose ricks and cottages were fired when the German aggressive force moved over their national boundary. The natural human desire of everyone involved in a catastrophe is to save his own possessions. Within the fighting area began to move those sad processions of refugees from the shelled and looted towns and villages, fugitives from burning homes laden with goods they sought to carry to safety. Beyond the

[1]See Note. [2]See Note.

fighting zone people rushed to shops to buy food, intending to hoard it; and there was the usual panic anxiety to withdraw money from the banks and to secure deeds and bonds.

In Britain the government acted promptly to avert panic. A *moratorium* was declared—a period of months during which no one might be compelled to pay debts. Producers and importers were required, by a quickly passed Defence of the Realm act, to hold their stocks as trustees for the nation, and sell them only as by law permitted. Competition between producers ceased; prices of all essential goods being fixed, by agreement. This arrangement suited the importers and producers, who were assured of selling at a profitable price, and contented the mass of the people. As stocks shortened, individual allowances of foods were tabulated, ration cards issued, and no one might buy more than his limited share. This share was calculated by a Food Control department of the government, after ample supplies had been reserved for the use of army, navy, and air force. Additional paper money was provided by the issue of Treasury notes of face value £1 and ten shillings. At the same time the gold coins in circulation were recalled; the holders were directed to exchange them at banks for paper money. It became an illegal act to receive gold in payment for goods.

The following were economic conditions in Britain immediately before the beginning of the World War:

1. Abundance of saleable goods; prices tending to fall.
2. Fierce national and international competition to sell.
3. Much abject poverty.
4. Shortage of purchasing power.
5. Increasing unemployment.
6. Discontent in industry; recent strikes.

Two years later we find:—

1. Surplus of goods nearly exhausted; prices rising.
2. Competition practically non-existent.
3. Less abject poverty.
4. A general increase of purchasing power.
5. No unemployment.
6. Maximum effort being made in industry.

At first sight it would seem that the war had benefited the British people who, but for two or three ineffective air raids, possessed their homes in peace, and suffered no immediate material loss. We shall see later whether this was actually the case. But how did it come about that when the reserve of goods was quickly wasting, and a shortage was beginning, there was *less* poverty and a general *increase* of purchasing power in the country?

The explanation is to be found partly in the war-time allowances paid by the government to the wives of combatants. Hundreds of thousands of men previously out of work or earning a pittance on which their families were underfed and ill-clothed, were now in the armies. Food and uniform cost them nothing, and their wives received a weekly sum of money for the support of their children. Never before the time of this war had the children in attendance at elementary schools been, as a whole, so well fed and clothed. Another source of purchasing power was the relatively high wages paid to women workers in munition factories, and to adolescent boys and girls filling in shops and offices the places of the men gone to the war front.

Most of the additional money in circulation was coming to the public through the various government departments as payment for goods and services connected with war-time needs. We have mentioned the issue of Treasury notes—but this was an emergency measure, intended to allay public anxiety and avert a tendency to panic at the war's beginning. The Treasury notes formed a very small part of the money spent by the government during the war years. The rest it borrowed, partly in credit from the Bank of England, partly from the public, which readily bought War Loan certificates and War Savings certificates, on which annual interest could be claimed. Credits were also obtained from American bankers. The National Debt rose until in 1919 it exceeded the colossal sum of £7,000,000,000, (seven thousand million pounds).

During the course of the war the greater part of this money was actually circulating, it was passing from hand to hand, paying for goods which were being consumed and for services which were being rendered. It was fulfilling the proper function of money, that of expediting the distribution of goods and the exchange of services. Therefore all classes were benefiting from its use, and even though the increasing scarcity of food made rationing necessary, acute poverty, virtual starvation, was banished.

Leisure was banished also. Men, women, boys and girls—all but the feeble—were turning full time energies either to production or to destruction. Neutral nations, the few not involved in the fighting, were producing at high pressure to supply the orders of the combatant nations. But the rate at which goods and munitions were consumed or destroyed overtook and passed the highest rate at which they could be produced. By the fourth year of the war nine millions of people had been killed, chiefly in Europe; hundreds of miles of pleasant country had been changed to a gas-poisoned waste whose soil would grow no crops, countless villages had vanished, many towns were in ruins. Supplies of food and clothing were short, raw materials for munition making becoming scarcer and dearer. Governments were coming to an end of their power to borrow more money.

The Russian army had been ill-equipped and badly organised from the start of the war. It was the tool of a weak and futile monarchy, which in 1917 was set aside by the *Mensheviks*, a Russian political party pledged to the support of a reformed Duma (parliament). Peace was made with Germany; and the Russians turned to the solution of their own problems—those of a wasted, debt-ridden people with a vast, ignorant peasantry scarcely above serf-level, of lagging industries financed by foreign credit-money, and of real wealth which was all in the hands of a relatively small class of landed proprietors. Before the end of this year KERENSKY, the Menshevik leader, was displaced by LENIN and TROTSKY, the leaders of the *Bolshevik* party, whose policy included the expropriation of private land and wealth, the end of capitalism, and the establishment of a Communist Russia. We shall refer to the development of this communist system in our next chapter.

In one more year the resources of Austria-Hungary, Germany and Turkey were exhausted—men-power, food and munitions. Those of France and her Allies had been renewed by the late entry of the United States of America into the war, but even in Britain the shortage was disturbing the government. Official posters urged people to eat the minimum of bread and to avoid waste of any description. In order to keep work-people contented bonuses of paper money were added to their wages—a form of inflation, since there was no possible corresponding increase in the supply of goods.

An armistice was signed on November 11th, 1918, as a prelude to peace. It was the virtual ending of the first World War.

CHAPTER IX

THE POST-WAR YEARS

BACK from the various war-fronts to their homes came the survivors of this international orgy of destruction. And when the medals had been distributed, and the shouts of welcome had died away, when men turned to take up their normal occupations—what were the economic conditions of the new peace?

In France, Belgium, Serbia, wherever actual warfare had been carried on, the consequent ruin and desolation precluded the immediate re-peopling of the area. The making of war cemeteries had to precede the rebuilding of villages. The poisoned soil, its fertility destroyed by absorption of foul gases, was obliged to undergo a long purification from sun, wind and frost before it could again feed the roots of growing plants. Elsewhere in the countries of the belligerent nations there was great need of constructional work; new building was four years in arrears, old buildings were lamentably in disrepair, roads wanted surfacing, and there was a shortage of vehicles of all kinds. Normal renovations had been long postponed, and there was a general appearance of shabbiness and decay. The men who returned from war with health and energy enough to enter into post-war activities thought to find work and wage easily, and looked forward to taking part in the building up of better homes and conditions. This was particularly the case in Britain—had not the Allies won the war!

Reconstruction! But though the need was evident

and urgent the work did not leap forward like a flame in the wind. There was a check to enterprise, an obstacle to progress, waiting round every corner.

The shortage of raw materials was soon remedied, except in the case of those that must be 'weathered'—like wood. But the shortage of purchasing power, which began to be felt again as soon as peace was made, was not remedied, for nearly everybody regarded it as inevitable. "We have spent enormously," the statesmen cried, "now we must retrench. We must amass money—we must save instead of spending. And all the people, rich and poor, must be encouraged to save too." This cry was echoed throughout the nations. Housing schemes, plans for new libraries, hospital extensions, municipal improvements, modern schools—all were dropped. Orders for goods were cancelled, the designs of the architects put aside. Reconstruction came nearly to a standstill.

In the case of the defeated nations, such saving seemed indeed essential. For the people of the Allies were demanding that their former enemies, the Germans in particular, should be compelled to pay dearly for making that initial move towards war, and for inaugurating the submarine campaign against merchant vessels. The Peace of Versailles required the German government to remit to the governments of Britain, Belgium and France a total sum of 136,000,000,000 marks—about six thousand eight hundred million pounds, besides consignments of coal and other goods. Instalments of this sum were to be paid annually, and it was assumed that the money would go far towards meeting the debts the Allies had incurred for war-time supplies; the latter peoples intended that the Germans should work hard and pay heavy taxes until the 'reparation' period was over and the goods and money delivered, while they, the Allies, benefited from German enterprise and endeavour.

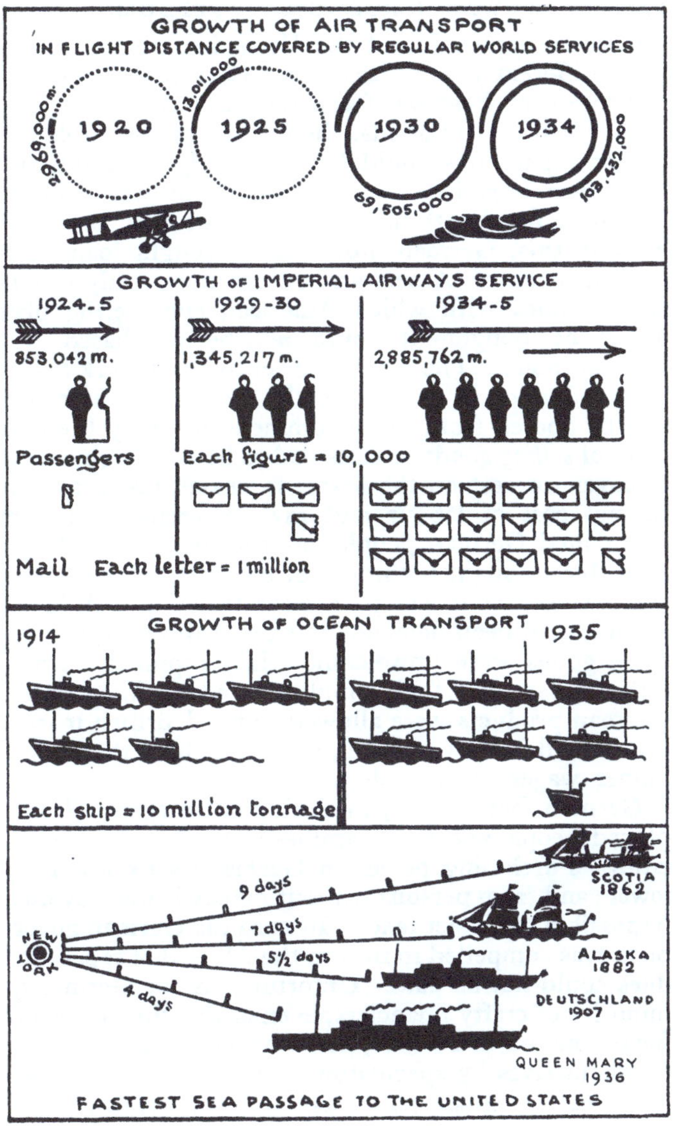
GROWTH OF AIR TRANSPORT
IN FLIGHT DISTANCE COVERED BY REGULAR WORLD SERVICES
1920
2,969,000 m.
1925
13,011,000
1930
69,505,000
1934
103,432,000
GROWTH OF IMPERIAL AIRWAYS SERVICE
1924-5
853,042 m.
1929-30
1,345,217 m.
1934-5
2,885,762 m.
Passengers
Each figure = 10,000
Mail
Each letter = 1 million
GROWTH OF OCEAN TRANSPORT
1914
1935
Each ship = 10 million tonnage
NEW YORK
9 days
7 days
5½ days
4 days
SCOTIA 1862
ALASKA 1882
DEUTSCHLAND 1907
QUEEN MARY 1936
FASTEST SEA PASSAGE TO THE UNITED STATES

But the application of the Versailles treaty resulted quite differently, as at least one wise British economist[1] had foreseen. Post-war Germany was a country drained both of money and goods. Before any considerable output of reparations could be produced, her industries, previously organised for the making of war material, had to be fitted with new plant for the new processes. To buy this, German industrialists sought loans from foreign bankers. American bankers were ready to lend credit-money with which American engineering plant might be bought—it could *not* be purchased with German notes. The plant was set up, and work began; but production in general for the German home market was hampered from its re-commencement by the difficulty of *selling* goods. Prices had to be kept high enough to cover interest on the loans, increased taxes, and the normal cost of labour and raw materials. The impoverished German people, stinting themselves to pay their dues, bought nothing they could possibly do without. Moreover it was soon clear that although 'goods in kind' had been demanded of the Allies by the treaty, these goods were unwelcome when supplied. British industrialists and their employees all declared that if German products were allowed to flood British markets prices in Britain would fall, and with them the hope of higher wages for British workmen.

German factories began closing down again. Unemployed people and their families starved in the German cities. Purchasing power in Germany sank lower and lower; and from persons without money it was obviously impossible to collect taxes. In 1922 the German government was compelled to inform the Allies that reparations dues could not be paid. Unfortunately for Germany, a minority of crafty financiers, even at this time of penury for the nation as a whole, had managed to amass money for themselves by speculation. Their names were well

[1]See J. M. Keynes, *The Economic Consequences of the Peace.*

known abroad, and their fortunes inclined the Allies to believe that Germans were trying to avoid the payments they had agreed to make.

Another factor which added to distress in Germany was the low value of money in circulation. Throughout the war years the quantity of paper money printed and issued to the public had *increased* as the quantity of goods *diminished* (exactly as in Britain) and the public effective demand for these goods had steadily raised prices. In 1913 twenty silver marks were worth an English sovereign—in 1919 both the silver and the gold money were gone from circulation, but German paper notes with a face value of 500 marks were worth no more in goods than the former 20 coins. And in the starvation years 1921 and '22 the value of the mark kept falling until paper money which might have purchased an estate in Germany two years earlier, would not pay for a single meal. Similar conditions obtained in Austria, in Hungary, and in smaller European states.

In comparison with the misery of the defeated peoples the experience of the Allied nations was merely that of increasing disappointment. The exultation over 'victory' soon died away; so did the hope of a general prosperity. As the demobilisation of the armies proceeded, the returning officers and men discovered that their country had small need of them. Work was being curtailed, and commercial and industrial staffs reduced, everywhere. The clerk or skilled artisan, fortunate enough to resume work at a post kept open for him during his absence, now dispossessed the war-time employee, and often found himself obliged to support similarly displaced sons and daughters—adolescents whose means of living had ceased with their war-time occupations. Nor were the young alone forced into unemployment. Sir Norman Angell says:—

"By the end of the year 1920 workers who on

numberless occasions had been told that their one salvation was to increase their output, and who had been upbraided in no mild terms because of their tendency to diminish output, were being discharged in their hundreds and thousands because there was a paralysing over-production and glut! Half a world was famished and unclothed, but vast stores of British goods were rotting, and multitudes of workers unemployed."[1]

We should note Sir Norman's exclamation mark. None knew better than he that there was no actual over-production at that date. What *was* happening was a world-wide falling-off of 'effective demand.' The unsold goods were needed no less than formerly, but people were unable to buy. Therefore production and commerce dwindled generally, and poverty spread. Even the citizens of the United States, who rightly prided themselves upon the vast real wealth of their country, and its capacity to supply more than their whole need, did not escape. The wheat and cotton farmers of the southern states had been producing chiefly for European markets, and not primarily for American ones. There were millions of American citizens whose households needed cotton goods, but these were poor wage-earners, as short of purchasing power as those in Great Britain. The demand from Europe, and especially from Germany, sank until plantation owners were faced with bankruptcy, and began to urge their government to make loans to German industrialists, so that they should be enabled to buy. But when this was done, the cotton planters only benefited, and temporarily, for when the Germans had made their cotton goods and tried to hand them over to their creditors the British and French, there was, as we have said, an outcry from the industrialists of those countries; while American indus-

[1] "The Fruits of Victory."

trialists, for similar reasons, insisted that a high tariff should keep cheap German goods from being sold in America.

We turn to Russia: this country has a different story. Before the war it was a great grain-producing land, 'the granary of Europe.' The Russian system of agriculture had been in some respects like that of the medieval manorial system described in Part I, Chapter VI—the land-holder having the first call upon the labour and time of the peasants, and the peasants living in the land-holder's village having rights over larger or smaller strips of communal soil. The revolution of 1917 dispossessed the aristocrat land-holders, and the peasants proceeded to divide up the land among themselves. They were, however, very ignorant and primitive folk, knowing scarcely anything of the world beyond their village, accustomed to direction from masters, and a narrow view of labour and organisation which the mere acquisition of more land did not widen. They could not at once change their habit of thought and action, and co-operate with the revolutionary leaders to replace the old system of society by a new and better one. Over wide areas in Russia trade and transport broke down altogether. Formerly the cities had received the greater part of the peasants' grain, and sent agricultural implements, clothing, sugar and other foods to the great estates; now the link with the cities was snapped. Peasants sowed little more than was necessary for their own needs.

Moscow, Petrograd,[1] and the other large cities suffered from food shortage; not only had normal supplies from the country ceased, but nothing was reaching them of all the imports sent in pre-war days from Germany, Britain and France. Most Russian factories were closed and derelict—they had been run

[1]Now Leningrad.

chiefly under foreign direction, and dependent upon foreign supplies of coal, steel, and machinery. All these supplies were stopped. The breakdown of the agricultural system, transport and commerce, resulted in the famine of 1921 and '22, when millions of Russians starved to death.

In 1920 LENIN, the Bolshevik leader, called together a committee of experts to consider a plan he had formed for producing electric power on a large scale, as the basis of industrial recovery. This was the beginning of the present Russian industrial system. American and British engineers were invited to Russia as teachers of engineering science; they helped to inaugurate in that country a new 'industrial revolution.' It differed from that of the 18th and early 19th centuries in two definite ways. There was no gradual change from peasant and artisan handicrafts to the marvellous achievements of high power machinery; instead, there was a leap from primitive processes to those made possible by one hundred and forty years of continuous invention and discovery.

The peasant and artisan learnt to make and use the most modern forms of labour-saving machinery. But they would use it under no terms of *laisser-faire*—there would be neither accumulation of private profit on the one hand, nor minimum wage on the other. The capital belonged to the State, not to individual owners or trading companies, nor would any such be permitted to make money fortunes by the sale of the product. Foreign markets would be sought, because by selling abroad the Russian government might obtain British, German or American credits, to be exchanged immediately for the necessary coal, steel, and those mechanical giants that by and by, when plant became available, should be born within the country.

The organisation of Lenin aimed at showing his countrymen how, by patient study and industry, they might build up an industrial system which should develop Russia's immense resources of real wealth, deliver them into the hands of the government for distribution, and ensure that sufficiency—even, in time, abundance, should be the right and possession of every citizen. This Communist experiment is proceeding: we cannot say yet whether it will lead ultimately towards economic freedom. At the time of writing a large part of Russia's energy is being diverted from the production of useful goods to the manufacture of war material.

CHAPTER X

RATIONALISATION

POST-WAR production and trade tended to pass into the hands of a smaller number of much larger companies; this was especially the case in America, Britain and Germany. As a result of war-time conditions many amalgamations had taken place, and many of the pre-war firms had closed down or been bought up by more fortunate competitors.

To the powerful organisers of the great companies it was becoming clear that a measure of co-operation in business would henceforth profit producers more than open competition. They met in consultation, they made joint agreements relating to prices and conditions of sale. They formed combinations known in Britain and America as *Trusts*, and in Germany as *Kartels*. In some cases a trust aimed at acquiring world-wide supplies of a particular raw material, controlling its sale and the sale of products into which it entered;[1] in others it gained possession of a sequence of related industries.

Such enormous organisations as the Trusts made it increasingly difficult for smaller concerns to continue working independently. The individual producer of extraordinary business acumen and capacity, such, for example, as Mr. Henry Ford, alone could hold his own against them. By the offer of high salaries and exceptional opportunities they attracted to their service the finest organisers, the most expert of chemists and engineers. These men became the brains of the Trusts;

[1]Such as the American Standard Oil Trust.

they subordinated human interests to 'big business' as, in the Middle Ages devoted Churchmen like St. BERNARD had subordinated such interests to the Church.

Behind the Trusts, and acting in conjunction with them, stood the great Banks. The latest development of capitalist enterprise was thus fully equipped, and able to command gigantic resources of both fixed and movable capital. By purchasing railway and shipping companies' shares a Trust could ensure special rights over transport; its wealth enabled it to buy the best factory and shop sites, and to make use of the latest mechanical inventions.

There were other forms of speculation in trade. Groups of financiers from time to time associated to make 'Rings' or 'Corners' in a particular commodity generally used by the public—wheat, for instance. They would instruct their agents to buy from the growers all the wheat readily available for sale over a certain area, with a view to raising the retail price above what this might have been if the growers had sold in open market. New, relatively small, companies were floated to supply novelties such as wireless sets, patent foods and drugs.

In Britain, suburban or village shop-keepers retailing household goods—food, clothing, drugs, coal, kitchen requisites—continued to make a precarious living in spite of the competition of the big stores. This was partly because the small trader would usually allow regular customers to have goods on account, while the rule of the stores was cash payment. But the life of the small trader was an endless struggle to obtain, on the one hand, saleable goods cheaply, and on the other to ingratiate himself sufficiently with needy customers to keep their custom and secure payment for their purchases.

Retailers of more durable goods found it profitable to sell on the 'hire purchase system.' This system was in working before the end of the 19th century, but on a small scale, and with some secrecy. The better class of employee still prided himself, in those days, on keeping out of debt. This pride was now, to a very great extent, disappearing. The widely-placed, attractive advertisements of the hire-purchase retailers easily induced wage and small salary earners to procure from them houses, furniture, cars, etc., at prices actually above the market value of the goods. Delivered upon receipt of a small first payment, these remained upon 'hire' until the last instalment of the price had been paid. Purchasers signed an agreement to pay a fixed instalment weekly or monthly; and young married people especially were ready to spend in advance the purchasing power which could only come to them as *future* earnings. They benefited from the use of the goods at the cost of a debt bondage which obliged them to accept any working conditions which would assure them continuous 'jobs,' and which added to the dread of 'unemployment.' Hitherto the poorer classes of wage-earners had had small chance of accumulating debts; they might now live in a state of more material comfort—with debt anxiety attached.

The development of the hire-purchase system also pointed to the fact that production was again outrunning consumption, as in the decade before the war. The inevitable result soon became apparent—prices fell. Everywhere the minority of people with ample means were furnished with both essential and luxury goods, except in cases where the government's cry for the practice of 'saving rather than spending' had influenced them to abstain. The majority of people were, it is hardly necessary to say, not so furnished, but they were buying goods to the limit of their purchasing power, or denying themselves necessaries in order to save.

Prices fell, and continued to fall. Producers were faced with a serious situation, threatening them with bankruptcy. If they had been able to see their problem as part of the larger one involving the fortune of humanity, they might have brought about a beneficial change in the financial and industrial system. But they could see no further than the immediate interests of their Trust, company or firm. Their thought ran on the following lines:

Ques. How may prices be raised?
Ans. By reducing the quantity of goods for sale.
Ques. How may the quantity of goods be reduced?
Ans. By inducing the government to place higher tariffs on those imported.

So high tariffs kept British and German goods out of the U.S.A., to the despair of the German producers. The French also 'protected' their home industries in this way, and even the British government eventually renounced its 'free trade' policy. By this means the volume of overseas trade from each country was further reduced, and British and Dutch shipping companies began to fail—becoming bankrupt because their ships could not find cargoes. Moreover, in spite of tariffs, prices tended still to fall.

Producers considered their position again. This time the argument ran something like this:

Ques. If, for the time being, it is impossible to raise prices, by what other means can we maintain a profit?
Ans. (a) By reducing our costs of working.
(b) By inducing the public to buy more of *our* goods.
Ques. And how can (a) be done?
Ans. By *Rationalisation*—the re-organisation of our works, stores, etc. on a labour-saving basis, with equipment of the most modern machinery. We shall

thus improve and increase the output of our product, and at the same time effect a reduction of our wage-expenditure.

Ques. What are the best means of achieving (b)?

Ans. By selling better goods at a cheaper price—our new machinery will enable us to do this; by advertising so widely that the name and excellence of our product will continually meet the eye and be dinned into the ear of the public.

Upon such suggestions as these producers acted. There was great inspection, great overhauling of departments, re-organisation of the factories, warehouses, stores, transport systems. Amazing new machines, the most recent inventions, took the place of a large percentage of the old staffs; sometimes from 50 to 75% of the former 'hands' were discharged. Those retained were required to work at a rate demanded by the regulated speed of the machines.[1] Many industrialists found that at this much faster rate more product than current sales disposed of was turned out in a five-day week; they therefore began to close their factories on the 6th day, thus further cutting down their expenditure on wages. A veritable wonderhouse was now the mechanised factory. Each movement timed to the second, completely co-ordinated with all other movements, almost frictionless, men and machine absorbed in motion—motion pouring out ceaselessly a fantastic wealth of goods. The power by which the machines were driven was generated by huge turbines.

"The largest single modern turbine has a capacity of 300,000 horse-power, or three million times the output of a human being on an eight-hour-day basis. But the turbine runs 24 hours a day[2]. . . .

Year by year as rationalisation proceeded, a more

[1]Satirised by Chaplin's film *Modern Times*. [2]F. Arkwright.

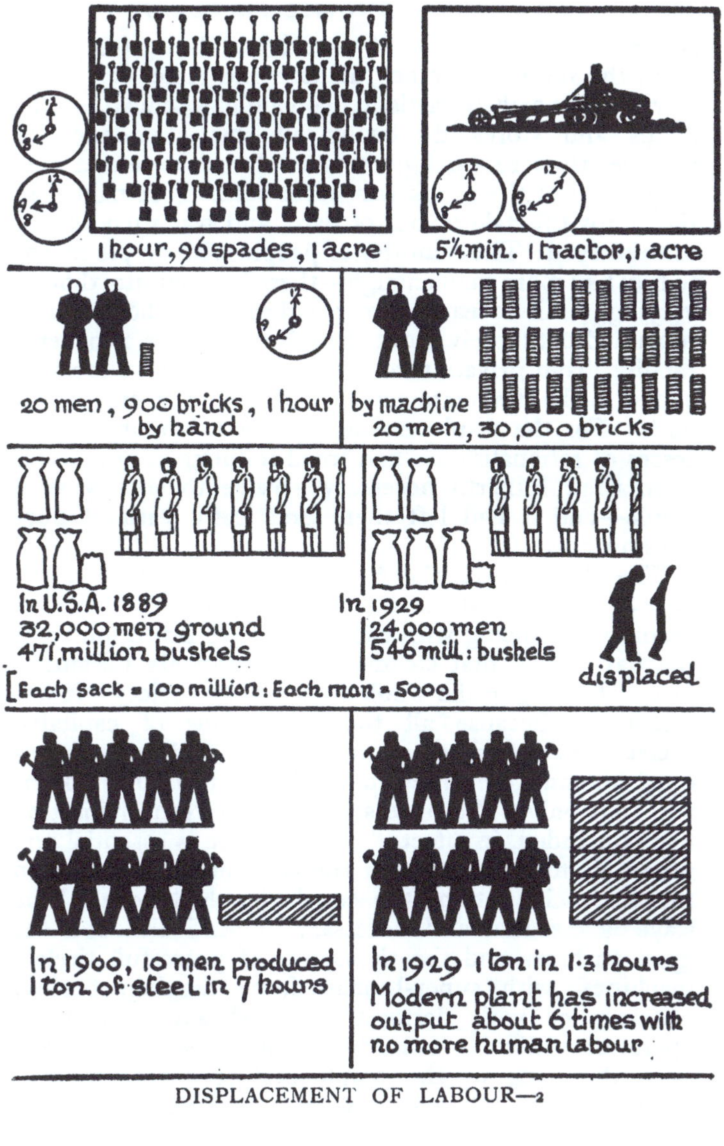

DISPLACEMENT OF LABOUR—2

super-abundant variety of useful and beautiful goods filled the marts of France, Britain and America. They were well-finished, artistic, convenient, cheap. The shops and stores displaying all this abundance of real wealth were a delight to see. But a large and ever larger part of the goods was never sold. It remained in the shops till stale or out of date, and was then wasted or destroyed. The minority of people with ample means to buy had more than enough—there is a definite, though varying, limit to each person's desires. The majority remained not merely unsatisfied, but in stages of poverty ranging from privation to the prolonged starvation that ended in the desperate acts of child-murder, suicide, or both. For the displacement of human labour by processes of rationalisation had freed millions of employees from their hitherto necessary service to society as a whole—and it had left them practically without purchasing power.

The change from the Age of Muscular Power to the Age of Mechanical Power, which had been slowly proceeding, advancing with each successive invention since the day of the first steam-engine, suddenly became a fact disturbing to the whole of capitalist society. It was disturbing because all the institutions of capitalist society, from Parliament downwards, had been developed in, and were suited to, an Age of Muscular Power, and that only. We have seen how western civilisation had concluded, in effect, "the employee is essential and necessary to the upkeep of the community," just as in the older civilisations the conclusion had been, "the slave is essential and necessary." And although the great turbines and the thousands of powerful, tireless machines, with super-human force digging, boring, heaving, or with deftness and delicacy performing operations difficult even to sensitive, skilled fingers, sang the song of the employees' freedom, western civilisation put its fingers in its ears and tried not to listen.

In America, in Britain, in France, in Germany, in Europe generally the people of wealth and leisure said: "Twelve millions of unemployed in the U.S.A., five millions in Germany, two and a half millions in Britain —how terrible! The governments *must* do something to put them back to work!" (In France the number was smaller because France's industrial population was relatively small, while greater, agricultural France was mainly in the hands of peasant farmers who used little power machinery.)

The unemployed themselves said, both personally and through their Trade Unions: "We want work! We claim the right to work! We don't want *charity*. The governments ought to give us *work*."

Two or three economists, who had studied the course of economic history and keenly observed the trend of modern industrial development, instead of memorising the theories of the classic economic authors, suggested that what the unemployed primarily needed was *money*. "Money to spend," said these modern thinkers, "on the goods the power-driven machines are providing for us all; on the goods that are spoiling and being deliberately destroyed for want of purchasers." The Spirit of the Time shouted them down with quotations from the classics. The leisured class declared the idea preposterous and dangerous—if the employed class were able to obtain money enough to support life in comfort without working they would relapse into complete idleness and probably drink themselves to death! The unemployed themselves muttered that they were respectable workers—they didn't want to be pauperised. The press treated the idea as current humour. Rationalisation, it announced, was bound to cause some temporary disorganisation. It was necessary to wait until things had settled down—until the expected revival of foreign trade put everything right!

In the meantime American charities distributed free

meals to a few hundreds out of the workless millions. The British government reluctantly paid out 'the dole' to its unemployed citizens. The 'dole' was a few weekly shillings from a State insurance fund to which the employee and his employer were each required to contribute weekly as long as wages were being received for work done. The dole kept a man and his family from starvation, but in a state of grinding poverty, half-nourished, half-clad, without opportunity or resource. Yet, miserable as it was, its recipients did not escape the suspicion of fellow wage-earners, who often heaped a partly envious scorn on dole-supported neighbours.

In Germany the millions of unemployed suffered no less because the *rentiers*—the class which depended on money received as rents and dividends—were suffering too. But the Germans all pointed to the Peace Treaty of Versailles, cursing its provisions, regarding the statesmen who made it, and the nations whose spokesmen the statesmen were, as responsible for their misery. They were largely right, but they did not realise that the Treaty itself was the fruit of past, but still potent, economic wrongs. The bottom cause of Germany's misery was Debt Accumulation. The Treaty had imposed the last, unbearable additions to Germany's load of war debts.

CHAPTER XI

BOOM, SLUMP, AND THE TRADE CYCLE

"TRADE is booming!" "A trade boom is overdue." The phrases are common—what do they signify? Promptly comes the reply: "An active state of business; an increase of effective demand; much buying and selling."

Periods of exceptional trade activity recurred during the 19th century, but each was closely followed by a slack period or 'slump,' when trade tended to dwindle, unsold goods accumulated, factories reduced staffs or closed down, industrialists and farmers went bankrupt. Certain commentators put forward the suggestion that this alternation of boom and slump followed natural law, like high and low tide, or day and night. This seemed feasible to many people, who henceforth recommended resignation to sufferers from the slump, since natural laws cannot be set aside.

There were, however, other persons disposed to inquire further into the matter. Clearly the circumstances most likely to cause a boom were increased public desire for goods, coupled with an increased supply of money to buy them. On the other hand a slump would be caused if, at a time when huge quantities of goods were being produced, the purchasing power of the public were suddenly lessened. But these simple alternatives were complicated and distorted by the part the operations of the 'money market' played in the business. The buying and selling of certificates of indebtedness—bonds, shares, bills of exchange, etc.—

and of the various national currencies in terms one of another; all such transactions affected both the quantity of money available to the public for buying goods, and the quantity of goods produced for sale. Yet more potently and directly did the issue and withdrawal of 'Bank-credit' in the form of loans encourage or depress trade.

Let us examine this last consideration—the part of the Banks in determining boom or slump. We have seen (Chap. IV) that bankers feel able to issue credit-money to eight or nine times the amount of the cash they hold. But they are under no law or obligation to create this maximum amount of credit, nor any part of it. They grant or deny loans as they please. Every thousand pounds of credit-money created assists the production, and should assist the distribution by sale, of one thousand pounds' worth of new goods. But consumers can only buy the goods if and when they receive wages, salaries and dividends (any or all of these) to the amount of one thousand pounds. Should the banker recall this loan (or any loan of equal value) before its equivalent has been distributed as purchasing power (w., s. or d.) there will be new goods placed on the market for which no new purchasing power is available. For, we must repeat, just as the 'loan' was created out of nothing, being merely a permission or authorisation to make impermanent money in cheque form, so it lapses, or becomes nothing, when cheques to the same amount are returned to the bank by the 'borrower.' The general tendency is, therefore, for trade to flourish when bankers are disposed to create money, and slacken when they destroy more than they create.

A useful comparison can be made between the conditions of the trade boom of the early eighteen-fifties and those of the most recent one, which affected the U.S.A. in 1928-29. The former began with the discovery of previously unknown gold deposits in Australia and America. Pioneer seekers made fortunes either by actually selling gold found, or by disposing of their 'claims' to hastily formed mining companies. In the neighbourhood of the gold-fields there arose an urgent demand for building materials, means of transport, everything ordinarily required for city construction and provisioning; this offered another chance for company promoters and the new shares were bought and sold wildly. . . . At the same time towns were rising in the American West and North-west, and there was railway construction going forward, both in that country and in Europe. All these conditions encouraged producers to expect heavy sales and high profits, bankers to create credit, and the investing public to buy shares. Confidence in the profitable nature of the enterprises led thousands of people to withdraw their savings from banks, or to sell shares in old, securely established companies paying small dividends, and to take up new ones promising greater returns. Necessarily this reduced bank deposits and, as a consequence, the possible supply of bank credit. Then came the day when the inflated prices of the shares would rise no higher, and holders began to appear anxious to sell. Public confidence was further shaken by the news that an insurance company had closed its doors owing seven million dollars; investors in other companies felt uneasy—and soon the whole tendency of bankers, investors, speculators, all the money market people, was to refrain from either lending or spending, and to sell, not buy.

Many thousands of firms were ruined in this slump. In modern industry the incapacity of one firm to pay its debts in due course may mean the failure also of its creditors, for if the banks refuse to make a loan to the embarrassed producer, he is without means to carry on. We have seen how the difficulties of the Bank of England Company were met by the British government in the 18th century; but the producer in difficulties can look for no government help in the form of Treasury notes or credit. In 1857 the Bank Act was indeed suspended, and the Bank printed an extra £2,000,000 worth of notes with a view to allaying the fears of the public, but only £928,000 of this new money was put into circulation. It did not prevent bankruptcies, with their dismal results, stoppage of useful and productive work, discharge of workers, decay of plant and buildings, the bringing to an end of enterprise. Such evils might have been avoided or mitigated, had not public opinion concluded them inevitable.

We pass to the year 1929. The U.S.A. is now the wealthiest country in the world, in terms of gold, of goods, and of potential production. Rationalisation has here gone forward more rapidly than in Britain.

In their capacity of general providers for the Allies during the war the Americans worked hard and sold as fast as they could produce, making good profits. Their entry as belligerents came too late to impoverish them as a nation. After the war their industry was kept busy meeting the needs of reconstruction in Europe. Exports from the U.S.A. to Europe, Britain included, went in enormous quantities, exports from Europe to the U.S.A. were relatively very small—so the gold stocks of the European banks (France excepted) crossed the Atlantic and were deposited in the vaults of the American banks. American producers and financiers grew so rich that they scarcely knew what to do with their money. They lent largely to the poor governments and industrialists of Europe, and especially, as we noted before, to the Germans.

> "This borrowed money was indeed for the most part applied to actual productive uses, though some of it was in effect *used to keep up the interest payments on European debts to the U.S.*"[1]

[1]G. D. H. Cole. *Money and the World Crisis.*

The words in italics show into what a desperately absurd position the world-wide practice of usury as a trading basis has led modern nations. The Germans were borrowing from their American creditors money to pay back to them as interest on previous loans! *Alice in Wonderland* can give us a situation no more absurd. We remember how, when Alice's comfits are distributed as prizes after the Caucus race, there is not one left for Alice herself. "But she must have a prize!" says the Dodo—and demands whether Alice has nothing else in her possession that will serve. Alice rummages in her pocket and produces a thimble, which the Dodo takes, and solemnly presents to her.

As rationalisation proceeded, public confidence increased, and high hopes were entertained of a general revival of world trade. True, there was more unemployment than there had ever been, but the general conclusion was, that when the revival came there would be work for all. Especially confident were the Americans, and especially sanguine the people of the Money Market. Bankers felt re-assured because Britain and other European states had 'gone back to gold.' This is a slang phrase, but the language of the Money Market is a jargon of slang terms peculiar to those who trade in money. The phrase means that the European governments had decided to make again (as before the war) the stock of gold bullion in the possession of their national banking companies the basis of their money issue. The quantity of paper money in circulation was to increase or diminish as the gold piled up or dwindled.

This does not mean that the value of the gold was to be represented exactly by the issue of the bank-notes, so that anyone might change his 'promise to pay' for a gold coin at will. The volume of money had grown immensely since 1914, but paper money had been printed and credit-money created much faster than gold or silver had been mined; there was not nearly enough of either metal to back the paper money of Europe.

In Germany the old, useless paper money had been replaced by a new, limited issue; money in that country was short, but the mark had at least a fixed value; and industrialism, sustained by the American loans, was making some progress. In Britain the Finance Act of 1925 had re-affirmed the Bank Charter Act of 1844; it had also decreed the withdrawal from circulation of the Treasury notes that had served so good a purpose during the war years and after. This process of *deflation*, being a reduction of the quantity of money in use, tended to reduce the prices of goods, and therefore of wages, but it also increased the demand for loans, and was on this (and other) accounts, welcomed by bankers. Its secondary effect was to reduce sales, but this was not immediately apparent. . . . Such an ancient, deeply rooted instinct is the trust in gold, such an emotion of security does its image invoke, that the very statement "Europe is back on gold," stimulated the Americans to a feeling of satisfaction and an optimistic faith in 'good times to come' that had no other foundation.

In the American industrial areas great preparations went forward for this expected world demand for products. New machines, new extensions to works, a tremendous appearance of prosperity! Investors began the usual rush to buy shares with intent to sell again at a profit while the boom lasted. Factory and shop sites were also bought and sold at high prices. Bankers and others who had invested money in Germany hurried to recall their loans and sell their German and Austrian shares, in order to trade with the money in New York where fortunes could be made in a week or two by the crafty speculator.

But the reality, below this appearance of prosperity, was to be seen in agricultural Europe and America. The majority of the farmers, the growers of wheat and

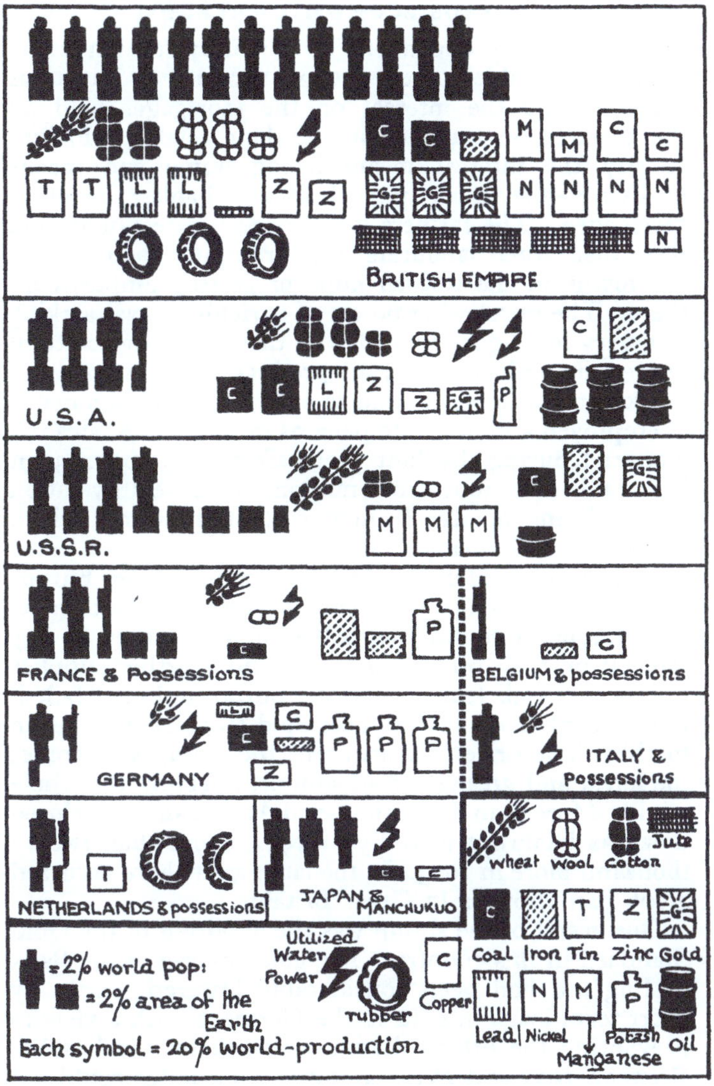

DISTRIBUTION OF NATURAL RESOURCES TO-DAY

cotton, formerly dependent on a mainly foreign trade, were now unable to sell enough produce to pay their expenses and the interest on the mortgages held by the bankers on the security of their estates. Failure to pay the interest meant losing home and means of living—the estate passed to the banker or other mortgagee. The farmers were in desperate plight, and their discharged labourers were tramping their way to the towns in the forlorn hope of getting employment there. The purchasing power of agriculture was sinking to a very low figure indeed, and that of the agricultural implement industry, and all producers of commodities for country use, was bound to sink too. The number of unemployed and destitute persons in the U.S.A. steadily mounted during the four years after 1929; by 1933 it had reached the fourteenth million. This wealthy nation was suffering no less from poverty than war-stricken, debt-ridden Germany.

The withdrawal of the American money from European industry was a further blow to production and trade. The Germans found themselves unable either to pay interest on their other loans, or to buy further supplies of raw materials from America. European banks failed. Public confidence in the forecasted trade revival began to ebb. The price of shares fell; the slump was come: the latest and greatest of all slumps, affecting the whole world. More than thirty thousand American firms closed down as bankrupt in the year 1932, more than twenty thousand more in 1933. In the latter year there occurred 4,606 bankruptcies in Great Britain.

One result of the slump was the abolition of the Gold Standard in this country. The gold reserve of the Bank of England had been considerably lowered, partly by short term loans in gold to the Germans with a view to preventing the utter collapse of Germany's industries. Between 1925 and 1931, although bank-notes could not be exchanged for gold coins at the Bank's counters, it was possible to buy gold bars weighing 400 oz. (it cannot be said that the majority of British subjects availed themselves of this permission) but since the latter year the Bank has not been legally obliged to sell. When the announcement was made that the Gold Standard had been abandoned there was national fear lest money should lose its value and notes become worthless as in Germany. But this fear soon proved groundless. There were goods in plenty; there were producers and traders eager to sell them. Within the country the abandonment of the Gold Standard made little difference to the exchange of goods; but abroad, at the counters of the exchangers, one could not get as many francs, marks, dollars, etc. for English money as before.

CHAPTER XII

THE APPROACH TO THE AGE OF LEISURE

WE have brought our tale down to the time in which we live; we must end this book with a summary and a forecast.

Men of the early civilisations lived precariously, insecurely. Shortage and want were the lot of the majority and the fear of all. Human communities were dependent upon local sources for their supplies, and upon muscular energy, human and animal, for the production and distribution of real wealth. Trade was the exchange of surplus goods. War enriched the victors and impoverished the vanquished. Gold and silver by weight were common, but not universal, measures of value. It was necessary that the majority of persons should work strenuously to maintain the community; by the labour of the many the few attained to leisure. These were the conditions of the Age of Scarcity.

Knowledge increased. The processes of agriculture and the crafts improved. Real wealth accumulated and with it came incentive to war. The importance of the king-leader and the military caste as defenders of the community's wealth grew, while that of the actual producers of the wealth seemed to take a second place. War progressively increased the slave population, slavery and the practice of usury resulted in further enrichment of the wealthy, and further impoverishment of the poor.

The great organising power of the Romans brought about heavier production, more effective transport, and vast accumulation of real wealth. But at the same time war and usury degraded to slavery or extreme poverty at least three-quarters of the people living in the Roman Empire. When the Roman system of government broke down, life in Europe again became sparse and simple, with low standards of agriculture, craftsmanship and individual wealth, but with little slavery. Between 1200 and 1700 standards of living and means of communication between peoples gradually improved—more generally in western than in eastern Europe. The Age of Scarcity conditions, however, still persisted, since no means of supplementing in any great degree the working power of muscular energy had been discovered.

Steam power was applied to industry in the 18th century. Its first effect was to speed up the rate of production of manufactured goods and also the rate of their transport. It became the ally of the capitalist system, displacing the handicrafts and substituting mechanical processes. The eventual result of the adoption of the capitalist system was the re-division of western communities into three main types of people—financiers, capitalist producers, and wage-earners. The application of electric power to industry (19th century) enormously accelerated the rate of production and delivered into the hands of the white races an almost unlimited measure of real and potential wealth. There followed a spate of invention, and a rise in the standard of living. For the first time in the world's history the economic needs of mankind as a whole could be more than met by scientific production. This fact was not immediately recognised. Well into the 20th century men continued to hold the Age of Scarcity principle that there must always be few satisfied and many in want. As a result of the general use of labour-saving machinery, a progressive displacement of human labour put millions of wage-earners at leisure—but left them moneyless and without means of living.

Money is anything used by the common consent of a community as a means of promoting the exchange of goods and services. Gold, silver and copper, being relatively indestructible, were adopted as money by the early peoples, and their use has persisted through the ages in leading civilisations. Coined metal succeeded metal by weight. Coins were struck by ruling authorities, royal or municipal, and by merchants of great reputation. By taxation the issuing authorities ensured a sufficiency of return to the royal or municipal treasury. From the 17th century onwards the immense growth of foreign trade made a less cumbersome type of money desirable, and gradually bankers' notes and credit were adopted as the means of exchange in the case of wholesale transactions, coinage being retained for retail trade and wage payments. This paper and credit money system, inaugurated by the Bank of England Company in 1694, spread with British trade throughout the world, and has given into the hands of international banking interests working for profit the supreme control of the creation and destruction of the means of exchange, and arising from this, the supreme control of production and trade.

Ours is the Age of Mechanism, the age of productive electric energy. The great natural force awaited for many thousands of years its discovery by the developing mind of man; in comparison with this long period, which we now call the Age of Scarcity, it is only yesterday since the potent discovery was made, and plenty for the race assured. Man is still in a state either of profound astonishment or of actual disbelief in the miracle that has taken place. "Every thought is a prison," said the philosopher EMERSON. The longer an idea is held the more binding it becomes, and we have accepted the inevitability of poverty and retained it too long to put it easily aside. The needs of the world's population can now be amply provided—indeed, *are* provided—and the poverty of to-day is an artificial and totally unnecessary condition. This it is essential we should realise.

The poverty of to-day is due only to the slow circulation and general shortage of money as purchasing power. A relatively small number of the public can buy to the full measure of their need. All the rest remain, in varying degree, unsatisfied. This is a transitory state of things; it can only continue while the general ignorance of real economic conditions lasts.

No human community would consciously assent to the deliberate destruction of its own prime necessaries, food, clothing and shelter. Yet such destruction, on a wholesale scale, is now being carried on, authorised by producers who cannot sell their goods.[1] Producers do not *wish* to destroy the fruits of their organising power. They wish to sell, and it is reasonable that they should be enabled to sell at prices which will cover the costs of their industrial or agricultural organisation and pay them for the exercise of their initiative and energy. The community wishes to buy, and would double, treble, quadruple its purchases if its members had reasonable means of obtaining money. But this is the point at which our present economic system fails—it provides no direct purchasing power.

All purchasing power is derived from some branch of industry, as wages, salaries, or dividends. The term 'dividends' includes profits from sales of all kinds. Pensions are paid out of industrial dividends or government taxes drawn from the earnings or dividends of the community. Before our time, the need for human labour in industry made compulsory the payment of a great annual aggregate sum in wages and salaries, most of which was spent at once upon goods; but year by year the installation of labour-saving machinery and electric power have reduced this sum, and with it the purchasing power of the community as a whole. The International Labour Office Report of 1933 showed a world total of thirty millions of registered unemployed persons. If we assume the low figure of two dependents for each of

[1]See Note.

these persons, we get a total of 90,000,000 of the world's population who were then necessarily at leisure, but without other purchasing power than an intermittent charity or the 'dole' afforded them. Yet, large as this total seems to us, it is small in comparison with the total of those persons still employed, or living at leisure upon tiny pensions, or belonging to that class of artists and professional people who love and follow an unprofitable vocation, whose lives are hampered and limited on every side by lack of money, the denial of the right to buy and consume a sufficient share of the waiting and wasting wealth.

On the one hand a majority of unsatisfied consumers —on the other such actual and potential abundance as the world has never before known. On the one hand a need amounting in the case of millions to virtual starvation; on the other the deliberate destruction of the food and other goods required. This is the situation to-day. These are the conditions of our approach to the Age of Leisure.

How long will that Age be delayed? Just as long as ignorance of economics remains general, and the ancient maxims of the Scarcity Age continue to pass for truth in the public mind. Just as long as Usury is permitted to function as the most indispensable of the professions. Until the statesmen of the world, truly representing the will of their respective nations, take control of Money, issuing and withdrawing it freely, not for the private profit of any man or section of men, but in accordance with its full and proper use as means to the exchange and rapid distribution of the world's fast-increasing wealth. Man has conquered Nature; it remains for him to conquer human greed, to grow wise in spending, to ensure to each individual his human right of choice and enjoyment, according to capacity, of all-abounding plenty; and to explore the infinite possibilities of a life of economic freedom and fruitful leisure.

APPENDIX I

NOTES

PART I

INTRODUCTION

Association for Labour. Agreement on the part of two or more persons to work mutually, with a view to reducing the difficulty of the work, finishing it in shorter time, and sharing the resultant benefit.

Division of Labour. Specialisation, which may mean:

(a) That the members of a primitive community divide among themselves the necessary labours, each performing that for which he is best suited—the community as a whole benefiting from the work of each member,

or (b) That the workers in a particular industry are divided into groups, each group being occupied in carrying out a part of the industry,

or (c) That in the complex manufacture of product the successive manufacturing processes are divided up among workers of whom each is engaged upon a single process. Thus, in the hand manufacture of cloth (See Pt. I, Chap. VI) the spinster, weaver, burler, fuller, rower, shearman and drawer deal in turn with the wool or fabric. In modern machine manufacture, labour is subdivided to such an extent that a worker may spend his whole working week repeating, momently or several times a minute, one small process such as tightening a nut, folding a sheet of paper, moving a lever.

CHAPTER III

Ephah. An ancient Jewish dry measure, estimated as approx. 8¾ galls.

Hin. The corresponding Jewish liquid measure; approx. 10½ pints.

Free Trade. Under a 'free trade' system goods enter and leave ports or markets untaxed. The prices to consumers therefore represent producers' and conveyers' charges only, as in the case of home produced goods.

Protection. Under a system of 'protection' imported goods are taxed on entering ports or markets. Consumers have to pay a price covering producers' and conveyors' charges plus this tax; the result being to make imported goods dearer than those produced at home.

The argument for 'protection' is that it tends to increase the demand for home products, thereby benefiting producers through additional sales and wage-earners by maintaining continuous work and wages. It also provides the State with a means of revenue. The argument against is that it reduces the quantity and variety of goods available for the general public, and by raising prices adds to the poverty of the poor.

Customs Dues and Tariffs. In early times and during the Middle Ages, an old custom was respected more than a new law. By such custom the king held the right to one cask in every ten of imported wines, and also to levy a tax on *exported* wool, hides, lead and tin. Later the term *customs dues* came to mean all taxes levied on imported goods,payable by importers before the goods could be placed upon the market. A *tariff* is a list of customs dues.

CHAPTER IV

Mortgage. In this case, the father, urgently needing money, had borrowed from a moneylender, giving as security the title deeds of the family homestead. The property was therefore 'mortgaged' to the money-lender, and became his possession if the borrower or his heirs failed to pay the yearly instalment of interest. The *mortgage deed* was the document setting forth the money-lender's claim on the property.

CHAPTER VII

Monopoly. The exclusive right to sell, or to restrain others from selling, a particular commodity.

Journeyman. The word *journey* originally meant a day's work or travel. The *journeyman* of the Middle Ages was the craftsman who had completed the period of his apprenticeship and was entitled to practise his craft and earn a wage in the employ of a master.

Capitalist. By *capital* we designate everything used by a producer in the production of goods. The hand-weaver's capital was his loom, his wool, and any money he may have put aside for the purchase of wool and for the repair, when necessary, of his loom. The word 'capitalist' came eventually to mean those owners of capital who employed non-owners, paying the latter a wage for their time and work.

CHAPTER VIII

Legal Tender. Anything which the law of the nation obliges a debtor to accept in payment of a debt. If A. owes B. for eggs, A. cannot oblige B. to accept the same number of eggs in payment, for eggs are not legal tender. Nor is B. compelled to accept a cheque, but can demand coin, or, if the debt is a large one, Bank of England notes.

"*The quantity of money in circulation increases while the quantity of goods for sale remains as before.*" A sudden increase in the amount of money circulating is called "an *inflation* of the currency." The 'currency' is a nation's 'current' or moving money—money passing from buyers to sellers, from employers to wage-earners, from shops and citizens to banks, from banks to bank customers.

It is useful to remember that:

(a) If the 'inflation' takes place when producers and shop-keepers are short of goods to sell, the sellers at once raise the prices of their goods. The general public has more money without being any better off in terms of real wealth.

(b) If an 'inflation' takes place at a time when warehouses are over-stocked with goods, and production is going on faster than consumption, the result will be to increase sales and to bring more real wealth into the hands of the general public. Prices will remain steady or slowly rise a little.

Tunnage and Poundage. The tax once payable on every tun of wine and every pound of merchandise imported into England. It was granted by Parliament to Edward III.

PART II

CHAPTER II

Income Tax. A tax on incomes was first levied by the English government of 1799. To-day a large part of the country's revenue is provided by income tax. As it is not a fixed amount, like a poll tax, but a percentage of income, the moneyed class pays more than the poorer. People with very small incomes are exempt from payment.

CHAPTER IV

Dividends. Yearly or half-yearly the accounts of all joint stock banks and trading companies are balanced—the total moneys expended are set against those received. If the income exceeds the total sum expended the firm has made a profit, and this profit is allotted according to the decision of the firm's directors. Unless the profit is very small (in which case it may all be retained for future expenses of the business) a *dividend* is declared—a division of profits among the shareholders. Holders of *preference* shares are given a larger percentage of profits than holders of ordinary shares.

(See the reports of company shareholders' meetings published on the financial pages of the daily press—particularly in January and July.)

Bank Rate. The current lowest rate of interest at which the Bank of England is prepared to make loans and advances (of created credit), and to discount bills of exchange. This rate is publicly announced by the Bank authorities each Thursday, and is adopted by the other banks.

Title Deeds. Legal documents certifying to the ownership of landed property. The owners of land, houses, mines, railways etc., keep the title deeds of such property, and must produce them before the proper legal authorities in the event of sale or other transfer of their holdings, or in case any dispute arises as to the ownership.

Bank Credit. The word 'credit' comes from the Latin 'credo' I *believe*; and the issue of bank credit is only possible because of the belief or confidence reposed in the banks by the public, and because of the mutual good faith that exists among business men generally. It is this confidence which makes it possible and natural for cheques (the visual form of bank credit) to function as money. As long as Producer A. is willing to accept Merchant B's cheque in payment for goods, no other form of money is necessary to ensure the transfer of goods from B. to A. Cheques have become the chief currency of the business world; the business man only *cashes* cheques—thus requiring notes and coin from his bank—for the purpose of paying wages to his workpeople, and for current expenses of a relatively small nature. Hence the total value of the legal tender money, notes and coin, is very small in comparison with that of cheque money used.

Banks of Issue. Those banking firms having the right to print and circulate bank-notes.

The Mint. The Bank of England Company purchases metals from mining companies, paying by cheque, and sends enough silver and copper to the Mint, for coining, to keep the banks supplied with 'change' for customers. Since coins are now used only for making small retail purchases, their total value is relatively small in proportion to that of the note and cheque money. . . . If we represent the whole value of English money, coin, notes, and bank deposits for the year 1933 as 50/-, the approximate value of the *coins* would be 1/-, that of the notes 9/- and that of the bank deposits 40/-.

CHAPTER VII

Joint Stock Companies. Originally persons lending money to the Bank of England Company received tallies as receipts. A tally was a strip of wood on which the amount paid was indicated by certain notches cut along its edges; after the record had been made the strip was split into two pieces, the lender retained the larger piece, called the 'stock', and the Bank the smaller, called the 'foil'. Hence the shareholders were said to hold 'bank stock', and this term was retained when written certificates of indebtedness replaced the tallies. Later it came to mean the share certificates of industrial companies also.

CHAPTER VIII

Interest-bearing Bonds. Certificates stating an obligation (on the part of an individual, a company, or a government) to repay certain loans after a named lapse of time, and in the meanwhile to pay so much per cent per annum as interest.

Creditor Governments. It is within the power of the statesmen entrusted with the disposal of the nation's revenue (in this country the Chancellor of the Exchequer and the Prime Minister, in consultation with the Governor of the Bank of England) to arrange for bank loans of credit to foreign governments. The intention, in time of peace, is generally to enable the debtor government to buy from the creditor nation goods needed for engineering projects; in time of war to purchase munitions and supplies of food. The interest on such loans becomes a charge on the taxes of the debtor nation.

The Russian Monarchy. Brought to an end by the revolution of 1917. The reigning family had been that of the house of Romanov, rulers of Russia from 1613. The last Czar was Nicholas II.

The Austrian Monarchy. The house of Habsburg, a royal line which ruled Austria from the 14th century until 1918, when, at the end of the World War, that country became a republic.

CHAPTER XII

Destruction of Goods. Between the years 1932 and 1935 the sabotage of food was common practice, it being done at the direction of the various associations of producers, or government-appointed Boards controlling industries. Some instances were as follows:

1933.

Brazilian coffee destroyed: 12,000,000 bags.

Oranges: a ship's consignment to Liverpool, arriving when the market was glutted, put overboard.

Sheep: large numbers slaughtered and carcasses burnt in the Argentine, South America.

Cattle: Slaughter of thousands for reduction of stock in Denmark.

Wine: 10,000,000 gallons wasted in Portugal.

Cotton: 11,000,000 acres of growing cotton destroyed in U.S.A.

1934.

Fish: The Great Yarmouth herring fleet's catch of some 15,000,000 herring returned to the sea.

Since 1934 the production of the more plentiful crops, farm-stock, etc., has been definitely restricted by agreement between governments and producers.

APPENDIX II

BIBLIOGRAPHY

ENCYCLOPAEDIAS

The Encyclopaedia Britannica.
The Jewish Encyclopaedia.
Encyclopaedia Sinica.

WORLD HISTORY IN OUTLINE

A Short History of International Intercourse, *C. Delisle Burns.*
The Story of Mankind, *H. Van Loon.*
The Living Past, *F. S. Marvin.*
The Outline of History, *H. G. Wells.*

ECONOMIC AND GENERAL HISTORY

The Dawn of History, *J. L. Myres.*
Human History, *G. Elliott Smith.*
Ancient Times, *J. H. Breasted.*
The Conquest of Civilisation, *J. H. Breasted.*
The Sumerians, *Sir L. Woolley.*
The Greek Commonwealth, *A. Zimmern.*
The History of Rome, *T. Mommsen.*
The Decline and Fall of the Roman Empire, *E. Gibbons.*
Companion to Roman History, *H. Stuart Jones.*
China: Her History, Diplomacy and Commerce, *E. H. Parker.*
A History of Egypt, *W. M. Flinders Petrie.*
Jewish Contributions to Civilisation, *J. Jacobs.*
The Economic History of Europe, *M. M. Knight.*
The Making of Rural Europe, *H. Douglas.*
The Economic History of England, *E. Lipson.*
An Economic History of England, *C. M. Waters.*
The Cambridge Medieval and Modern Histories.

SPECIAL AND PERIOD HISTORY

Historia Numorum, *B. V. Head.*
A History of Sanscrit Literature, *A. A. Macdonell.*
Villeinage in England, *Sir P. Vinogradoff.*
Six Centuries of Work and Wages, *T. Rogers.*
English Farming, Past and Present, *R. E. Prothero.*
The Town Labourer, *J. L. & B. Hammond.*
The Village Labourer, *J. L. & B. Hammond.*
The Skilled Labourer, *J. L. & B. Hammond.*
English Industries of the Middle Ages, *L. F. Salzmann.*

Town Life in the Fifteenth Century, *A. S. Green.*
A History of Everyday Things in England, *M. & C. B. H. Quennel.*
A History of Taxation & Taxes in England, *S. Dowell.*
The First Nine Years of the Bank of England, *T. Rogers.*
A History of the Bank of England, *A. Andreades.*
The Industrial and Commercial Revolutions in Gt. Britain during the 19th Century, *L. C. Knowles.*
The Century of Hope, *F. S. Marvin.*
Life and Labour in the 19th Century, *C. R. Fay.*
Past and Present, *T. Carlyle.*
The History of Trade Unionism, *S. & B. Webb.*
The Life of Robert Owen, *R. Owen.*

Economic Theory
A History of Economic Thought, *L. H. Hancy.*
An Enquiry into the Nature and Causes of the Wealth of Nations *Adam Smith.*
Principles of Political Economy, *D. Ricardo.*
An Essay on the Principle of Population, *T. Malthus.*
An Explanation of the Distress which pervades (1816) the Civilised Parts of the World, *R. Owen.*
The Theory and Practice of Banking, *H. McLeod.*
Capital, *K. Marx.*

20th Century Economic History & Theory
British Trade & Industry, Past & Present, *G. D. H. Cole.*
Modern Money, *Lord Melchett.*
The Control and Distribution of Production, *C. H. Douglas.*
Real Wealth and Financial Poverty, *W. Adams.*
The War and Employment, *A. L. Bowley.*
Prices & Wages in the United Kingdom 1914-20, *A. L. Bowley.*
Losses of Life Caused by War, *S. Dumas & K. Petersen.*
The Economic Consequences of the Peace, *J. M. Keynes.*
The Fruits of Victory, *Sir N. Angell.*
War Debts and Reparations, *G. D. H. Cole.*
War Finance, *J. S. Nicholson.*
Social Credit, *C. H. Douglas.*
The Intelligent Man's Guide Through World Chaos, *G. D. H. Cole.*
The Modern Idolatry, *Jeffrey Mark.*

INDEX

MADE AND PRINTED IN GREAT BRITAIN BY
EBENEZER BAYLIS AND SON, LTD., THE
TRINITY PRESS, WORCESTER, AND LONDON